D0968807

"Then **Ditka** Said to **Payton**..."

The Best Chicago Bears Stories Ever Told

Dan Jiggetts and Fred Mitchell

TRIUMPH
BOOKS

Library of Congress Cataloging-in-Publication Data

Jiggetts, Dan, 1954–
Then Ditka said to Payton—: the best Chicago Bears stories ever told / Dan Jiggetts and Fred Mitchell.
    p. cm.
  ISBN-13: 978-1-57243-985-6
  ISBN-10: 1-57243-985-8
1. Chicago Bears (Football team)—History. I. Mitchell, Fred. II. Title.
GV956.C5J54 2008
796.332'640977311—dc22
                                                    2008009231

This book is available in quantity at special discounts for your group or organization. For further information, contact:

Triumph Books
542 South Dearborn Street
Suite 750
Chicago, Illinois 60605
(312) 939-3330
Fax (312) 663-3557

Printed in U.S.A.
ISBN-13: 978-1-57243-985-6
Design by Patricia Frey
Photos courtesy of Getty Images unless otherwise indicated.

I dedicate this book to my parents, Floyd and Hattie Jiggetts, for giving me life and for always being there. I miss you dearly. And to all of my former teammates who provided me friendship and fond memories.

—Dan Jiggetts

This book is dedicated to my parents, LeRoy and Esther Mitchell, for all of their encouragement, and for introducing me to the worlds of sports and journalism that have meant so much to me. And to my wife, Kim, for your patience and love.

—Fred Mitchell

table of
contents

acknowledgments

Special thanks to the *Chicago Tribune* sports department, including assistant managing editor/sports Dan McGrath, sports editor Mike Kellams, and assistant sports editor Ken Paxson; Alan Peters from the *Tribune's* research department; Triumph Books editors Tom Bast, Mike Emmerich, Adam Motin, and Morgan Hrejsa; and to the Chicago Bears.

The following resources were used during the research and writing of this book:

ChicagoBusiness.com
ChicagoSports.com
ProFootballHOF.com
ProFootballReference.com
SI.com
SportingNews.com
TheHistoryMakers.com
USAToday.com

chapter 1
The Start of Something Big

Bears great Red Grange was one of the first superstars in pro football history.

It's been more than 85 years since the embryonic stages of Chicago Bears development, but the history lessons here deserve the devoted attention of every serious sports fan. So pull up a chair next to the fireplace and let us take you back to a time in the NFL when the forward pass, salary cap issues, and television timeouts were a mere twinkle in the eyes of the league's founding fathers.

The Birth of the Bears

The Bears, as we know them today, were conceived as the Decatur Staleys in 1920. A man named A.E. Staley, who owned the Staley Starch Works company in Decatur, Illinois—about 200 miles southwest of Chicago—hired George Halas as recreational director to coach a football team. Dutch Sternaman helped coach that team.

In 1919, the company had fielded a club football team. Halas, a would-be starch maker during the day, was hired to reorganize the Staleys football team as well as establish baseball and basketball teams. A man named George Chamberlain made the phone call to Halas on behalf of the Staley Starch Company. Chamberlain, who was aware of Halas's numerous accomplishments, wondered whether he would be interested in taking a job with his company.

To this point in his life, Halas had already played college football at Illinois, participated in the military in World War I, and played for the Great Lakes Naval team that won the 1919 Rose Bowl, where he was named the game's MVP. Not too shabby.

Indeed, Halas accepted the offer from Chamberlain and made his way down to central Illinois.

According to league records, the Staleys opened their 1920 season with a 7–0 victory over the Rock Island Independents, followed by another shutout, 10–0, over the Chicago Tigers. Their third game, also against the Rock Island Independents, wound up in a scoreless tie. The Staleys routed the Hammond Pros 28–7 and beat the Chicago Tigers again 6–0 before suffering their only loss of the season, 7–6, to the Chicago Cardinals. They rebounded by exacting revenge against the Cardinals with a 10–0 triumph the following week. Their season concluded with a scoreless tie against the Akron Pros. Among the key players on that Staleys roster were Sternaman, Hugh Blacklock, George Trafton, and Guy Chamberlain.

At the conclusion of that inaugural season, Halas then traveled to Canton, Ohio, for a historic meeting with other professional team owners. From that rather casual meeting was born the American Professional Football Association, which would later be renamed the National Football League. There were no ESPN cameras or NFL Network filmmakers in attendance at this meeting—just several earnest men who relied on the integrity of a handshake. And a small amount of cash, of course. Each organization had to come up with $100 to join the league.

As the fledgling team struggled financially in Decatur, Staley eventually gave Halas $5,000 and advised him to move the club

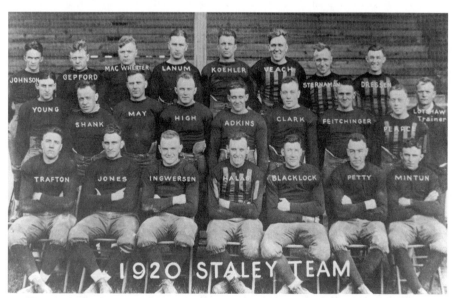

The Decatur Staleys were formed in 1920. They later moved and were renamed the Chicago Bears.

to Chicago. The name Staleys had to be retained for at least one year; that was the only caveat. With the team uniforms and seed money in hand, Halas also agreed to provide free advertising in game programs for Staley Starch Works.

The next question: where would the Staleys play in Chicago?

Halas arranged to lease Wrigley Field from Bill Veeck Sr., then-owner of the Chicago Cubs. Since Halas was a former baseball player himself, and a huge Cubs fan, the name Bears seemed natural. (Cubs...Bears, get it?) So the team changed its name to the Bears in 1922.

The start of one of the most intense rivalries in all of sports began in 1921. That's when the Green Bay Packers joined the AFPA, while the Chicago Staleys finished with a record of 9–1–1 and were named league champions. It is not clear whether the Packers were referred to as the Cheeseheads back then, but the football border war was off to quite a start.

In 1922, Halas acquired Hall of Fame tackle Ed Healy from the Rock Island Independents. The team would never be the same.

Red Grange, the NFL's First Star

As you might imagine, the NFL was struggling financially in those early days. With no television and little publicity, the league really needed a boost. That's when Halas figured he needed to snare the biggest name in college football—Harold "Red" Grange. A native of Wheaton, Illinois, "the Galloping Ghost" was breaking all of the college records at the University of Illinois. Halas signed Grange just as soon as his Illini eligibility was completed. The crowds started to follow the biggest name in college football, and pro football was beginning to take center stage.

The first attempt to draw more fans with Grange as the gate attraction was on Thanksgiving Day, 1925. Just 10 days after Grange's last college game, 36,600 fans packed Wrigley Field to see Grange's pro debut against the Chicago Cardinals. Just 10 days later, more than 70,000 crammed into New York's Polo

Grounds to see Grange and the Bears take on the New York Giants.

The idea of bringing Grange into the pro football fold was paying dividends to everyone involved. Grange's agent, C.C. "Cash and Carry" Pyle, wasn't about to miss out on this chance to cash in big time. To that end, Pyle, Halas, and Sternaman lined up an exhausting 17-game barnstorming tour of the country, attracting thousands of new fans for pro football.

The barnstorming tour took them across the country, from New England to Florida, then to the Pacific Northwest. The Bears played 17 games in 45 days, and Grange and his agent pocketed more than $100,000 from the tour.

But when Pyle and the Bears couldn't agree on contract terms (sound familiar?) for the 1926 season, Pyle formed the rival

Red Grange helped put professional football on the map during his years with the Bears.

American Football League with a team in New York called the Yankees. His new team would feature Grange.

In the short term, the Yankees had moderate success, but the rest of the league failed. Pyle was allowed to move his Yankees team into the NFL in 1927, but Grange suffered a devastating knee injury during a game against the Bears, of all opponents.

"I didn't play at all in 1928," Grange was quoted as saying following his storied football career. "I was just an ordinary ball-carrier after that. I did develop into a pretty good defensive back, however."

Always in need of exceptional player talent, Halas invited Grange back to the Bears in 1929, and he remained with Chicago through the 1934 season. In fact, Grange showed off his defensive prowess in the 1933 NFL Championship Game. He made a clutch touchdown-saving tackle in the final seconds.

With no surprise to anyone who had followed the game back then, Grange became a charter inductee to the Pro Football Hall of Fame in 1963. Grange died January 28, 1991, at the age of 87.

George Halas, Ageless Wonder

During his career, George Halas retired three times, first in 1929, then again in 1942 (because of World War II), and once again in 1955. But each time he kept coming back to coach.

An example of Halas's great sense of timing—or was it simply fate?—was the 1915 capsizing of the *Eastland* passenger ship. He had worked temporarily for Western Electric and was planning on being on that particular *Eastland* voyage. Halas was running late, however, and missed the capsizing that sadly took the lives of 841 passengers and four crew members.

The city of Chicago held a strong significance for Halas, who graduated from Crane Tech High School. He played football for head coach Bob Zuppke at Illinois, as well as baseball and basketball. He earned a degree in civil engineering while helping Illinois win the 1918 Big Ten football title.

During World War I, Halas served as an ensign in the navy, and he played for a team at that Great Lakes Naval Training Station that won the 1919 Rose Bowl. The team included future Pro Football Hall of Famers Paddy Driscoll, who once drop-kicked a 50-yard field goal, and Jimmy Conzelman. Halas scored two touchdowns and returned an intercepted pass 77 yards in that 17–0 Rose Bowl victory. Players on that 1919 team were also rewarded with their military discharges.

Not fulfilled by the success of his amateur football career, Halas played minor league and semipro baseball. He was even promoted to the major league New York Yankees, where he played 12 games as an outfielder in 1919. But a hip injury ended his baseball career.

Conzelman was also a key figure in the early development in what would become the National Football League. He had been a halfback at tiny Washington University in St. Louis before he became a teammate of Halas's on that Great Lakes navy team. Halas then recruited Conzelman to play for his Decatur Staleys.

After one season with the Staleys, Conzelman moved on to the Rock Island Independents and began his career as a player/coach. He stayed with the Independents through seven games of the 1922 season before jumping to the Milwaukee Badgers for the remainder of that season and all of the 1923 and the 1924 seasons.

In 1925, Conzelman was offered an opportunity to become an NFL owner for a franchise in Detroit. The cost? One hundred dollars. My, how times have changed. He took the deal. Conzelman's team performed well on the field (8–2–2 in 1925) but received little fan support from Detroit fans.

Because of the poor cash flow, Conzelman eventually returned the franchise to the league and in 1927 joined the Providence Steam Roller as player/coach. He suffered a knee injury in 1928 while playing quarterback, ending his playing days, but he managed to coach the team to an 8–1–2 record and the NFL title.

In 1940, Conzelman returned to the NFL with the Chicago Cardinals during the war years. Then he went to work in Major

League Baseball briefly. In 1946, Conzelman returned to the Cardinals and they won the NFL title a year later. He was inducted into the Pro Football Hall of Fame in 1964.

The Bears finished with a losing record (4–9–2) in 1929 for the first time in their history. Following that season, Halas and Sternaman hired former Illinois assistant Ralph Jones to become their new head coach. At that time Jones made a promise to Halas that he intended to keep—he said he would return the Bears to the championship in three years.

It didn't take him that long. Jones delivered by guiding the Bears to another world title in 1932. Halas again became head coach of the team in 1933, and the Bears won yet another title.

The first NFL draft was held in 1936, but it was the 1939 NFL Draft that proved particularly fruitful for the Bears. Halas selected future stars in Sid Luckman, Bill Osmanski, and Ray Bray that year alone.

Innovation on Offense and a Change in Ownership

The Bears became the first team to become truly innovative on offense by lining up the quarterback directly behind the center. They also decided to have their offensive linemen space out a little more in order to open up holes for their backs. They even devised blocking schemes and fake runs that turned out to be jump passes.

The new-look Bears finished 9–4–1 in 1930. They whipped Green Bay in the season finale, but the Packers were awarded the league championship because of their better overall record.

In 1931, the Bears were 8–5, but during that off-season Sternaman wanted out as co-owner of the team. He was feeling the pressure of the Great Depression, and Halas was forced to scramble for the $38,000 needed to buy out Sternaman's share. According to the fine print, if Halas did not come up with the money, full ownership of the team would revert to Sternaman at noon on August 9, 1932.

Halas later told biographers that he thought the fine print in the contract was merely "legal hocus-pocus," but when August 9 came around, he discovered he was $5,000 short of the payment to Sternaman and out of resources.

Halas was disconsolate and coming to the realization he might very well lose his Bears. But at 11:00 AM, C.K. Anderson, president of a bank in Antioch, Illinois, saved the day for Halas. He called and agreed to loan Halas the remaining $5,000. Halas had just enough time to get the money and run to the office of Sternaman's lawyer.

The Bears began the 1932 season inauspiciously with three ties and a 2–0 loss to Green Bay. But the Bears rallied and after beating the Staten Island Stapletons 27–7 on October 23, they finished the regular season 6–1–6.

The Bears were set to host the Portsmouth Spartans (later to become the Detroit Lions) for the NFL championship in 1932. Because of brutal Chicago weather, the two teams agreed to play the game inside Chicago Stadium. The Bears had also played an exhibition game in Chicago Stadium in 1930. It might have been a better place to play than outdoors, but fans and players had to hold their nose. Playing on an 80-yard indoor field filled with mud and animal manure because the circus had been held there, the Bears prevailed 9–0 over Portsmouth, which was without its star quarterback, Dutch Clark, because he was scheduled to start his off-season job.

After keeping his promise to Halas that he would bring him a championship within three years, Jones left the Bears in 1933 to become the athletics director at Lake Forest College. The Bears repeated as champions in 1933, defeating the New York Giants 23–21 at Wrigley Field in the championship game.

The Bears were perfect in 1934, going 13–0. That Bears team held the NFL record for most consecutive victories (18) until it was broken during the 2004 season by the New England Patriots. In the 1934 championship game rematch with the Giants, this time at New York, the Bears succumbed 30–13. The game was played on an ice-coated field, and at halftime the Giants changed to running shoes, which they felt gave them better traction than cleats. After the loss, Halas vowed never to get caught short without a change of shoes available for his players.

From 1935 to 1938, the Bears were 30–13–3 but didn't win any championships. Grange had retired following the 1934 season. The legendary Bronko Nagurski left after 1937, and the team also lost Bill Hewitt and Beattie Feathers, the first running back in history to rush for 1,000 yards in a season.

For the 1938 and 1939 seasons, Halas hired University of Chicago head coach Clark Shaughnessy, regarded as an offensive mastermind. Under Shaughnessy the Bears changed their attack and adopted the classic T formation. The Bears refined the formation that had been previously used to some extent in colleges and the pros. That's when the Bears really took off. They won championships in 1940, '41, '43, and '46. The Bears' record during this era was 223–76–33 as they began to earn their storied nickname as Monsters of the Midway.

Sid Luckman, who would star for the Bears from 1939 to 1950, still holds many of the franchise's passing records. He led the Bears to four NFL championships during that period. Born in Brooklyn to Jewish German immigrants, he played both baseball and football for Erasmus Hall High School and Columbia University. At Columbia, he completed 180 of 376 passes for 2,413 yards and 20 touchdowns. He finished third in the 1938 Heisman Trophy voting, losing to Davey O'Brien and Marshall Goldberg. He was voted into the College Football Hall of Fame in 1960.

In 1942, the Bears posted a perfect 11–0 record and outscored their opponents 376–84. Luckman was the mastermind, completing 54 percent of his passes and executing the offense to perfection.

The most resounding victory in an NFL Championship Game occurred in 1940, when the Bears blasted the Washington Redskins 73–0.

The Bears had opened the 1940 season with a 6–2 record. After they lost 7–3 on November 17 in Washington, Redskins owner George Preston Marshall was quoted in the paper as calling Halas and his Bears "front-runners," "quitters," and "crybabies."

That was all Halas needed to hear to get his troops psyched up for the rematch. Even in those days, inflammatory words such as those became bulletin board material. It was payback time!

The Bears would score 78 points in their final two regular-season games. That set up the championship game showdown in Washington on December 8. Prior to the game, Halas distributed clippings of Marshall's comments to his players and said, "Gentlemen, this is what George Preston Marshall thinks of you. I think you're a great football team, the greatest ever assembled. Go out on the field and prove it."

Bill Osmanski swept the left side and scored on a 68-yard touchdown just 55 seconds into the game, and the rout was on. The Bears would score so many touchdowns that, late in the

Bill Osmanski and the Bears crushed the Washington Redskins 73–0 in the 1940 NFL Championship Game.

game, the officials implored Halas to have his team run for the extra points. That was because they were running out of footballs that had soared through the uprights and into the crowd.

In the end, the score was 73–0, the largest margin of defeat in NFL history. Luckman passed only six times, with four completions and 102 yards in the rout. But that win was the beginning of more than six years of Bears dominance of the NFL. From 1940 to 1946 the Bears played in five NFL Championship Games, winning four, and they posted a 54–17–3 regular-season record.

The Bears finished 10–1 in 1941, losing only to the Green Bay Packers, and by only two points at that. In a playoff game prior to the NFL Championship Game, the Bears paid the Packers back, winning 33–14. Then a second championship in a row was secured for Chicago with a 37–9 victory over the New York Giants at Wrigley Field. That game was played two weeks after the Pearl Harbor attack.

Following an October 25, 1942, victory over Philadelphia, Chicago's 12th victory in a row, Halas turned his team over to assistants Hunk Anderson and Luke Johnsos and entered the navy for a tour of duty in the Pacific theater. The Bears would win the final six games that season, giving them 18 straight wins, but they lost the 1942 NFL Championship Game 14–6 to the Redskins.

The Legends of the 1940s

In 1943, former star fullback Bronko Nagurski was coaxed back onto the team to play one final season. He played the season mostly at tackle, but also played fullback before the year was over.

He was born Bronislau Nagurski in Rainy River, Ontario, Canada, and his family moved to International Falls, Minnesota, on the Canadian-U.S. border when he was still a boy. His parents, Mike and Emelia Nagurski, were immigrants, ethnic Ukrainians from the Polish Ukraine (Galicia). Nagurski became a standout at the University of Minnesota, where he played fullback on offense, tackle on defense, and was named an All-American.

According to legend, Nagurski was discovered and signed by a University of Minnesota athletics officer who had gotten lost and asked for directions to the nearest town. Nagurski, who had been plowing a field without a horse, lifted his muddy plow and used it to point in the direction of town. He was signed on the spot for a full-ride football scholarship.

In 1929, Nagurski was a consensus All-American at tackle and also made some All-American teams at fullback. Perhaps his greatest collegiate game was against the Wisconsin Badgers in 1928. Wearing a corset to protect cracked vertebrae, he recovered a Badgers fumble deep in their territory and then ran the ball six straight times to score the go-ahead touchdown. Later in the same game, he intercepted a pass to seal the victory. During his time with the Gophers, the team went 18–4–2 and won the Big Ten championship in 1927.

Sports Illustrated named Nagurski one of the three greatest athletes in Minnesota state history. The other two were Dave Winfield and Kevin McHale. In 1993, the Football Writers Association of America created the Bronko Nagurski Trophy, awarded annually to the best defensive player in college football. Notable winners include Warren Sapp, Charles Woodson, Champ Bailey, and Derrick Johnson.

Nagurski retired from pro football in 1937 after eight seasons to pursue a more profitable pro wrestling career. He returned to the Bears in 1943 when the team was short of players during World War II. He is 10th on the Bears' all-time rushing list.

Sid Luckman enjoyed his finest season in 1943, completing 110 of 202 passes for 2,194 yards and 28 touchdowns. During one game that year, Luckman threw for 443 yards and seven touchdowns, still tied for the most passing TDs in one game. He led the Bears to championships in 1940, 1941, 1943, and 1946. Luckman also had 132 interceptions in his career.

One of several key Bears players in the 1940s was Hall of Fame halfback George McAfee. He was just 6'0" and 178 pounds, but, man, could he run.

After being drafted by the Philadelphia Eagles, Halas traded for the Duke All-American in 1940, and McAfee turned out to be a terrific two-way performer. He scored 234 points, gained 5,313 combined net yards, and intercepted 25 passes in eight seasons. He was also the NFL punt return champion in 1948, and his

Hall of Famers George McAfee (left) and Sid Luckman were a dynamic duo for the Bears of the 1940s.

career punt return average is 12.8 yards. A member of the 1966 Pro Football Hall of Fame class, McAfee returned a punt 75 yards for a touchdown with just seconds remaining to defeat the Brooklyn Dodgers in his first exhibition game.

In the 1940 regular-season opener, McAfee ran back a kickoff 93 yards and threw a touchdown pass in a 41–10 Bears victory over rival Green Bay. In the historic 73–0 rout of the Washington Redskins in the 1940 NFL Championship Game, McAfee contributed a 34-yard interception return for a touchdown. McAfee's pro career was limited to just eight years before and after World War II service. He was a breakaway runner, a dangerous pass receiver, and one of history's best kick-return specialists as evidenced by his record-breaking punt return average. He was known as "One-Play McAfee." He also pioneered the use of low-cut shoes, which he believed improved his speed and elusiveness.

Another significant player of that era was Clyde "Bulldog" Turner. Turner excelled as a center and linebacker for the Bears. He was drafted by the Bears in 1940 and was a rookie starter at the age of 20 following a Little All-America career at Hardin-Simmons. Legend has it that a Hardin-Simmons fan tipped off Frank Korch, a Bears scout, about Turner's abilities during his junior season. After watching Turner, Korch convinced Halas the Bears should draft him. Meanwhile, the Detroit Lions were so sure they had convinced Turner to turn down offers from other NFL teams they didn't even bother to draft him.

At 6'1", 237 pounds, Turner had halfback speed. He led the NFL with eight interceptions in 1942 and totaled 17 interceptions over his career. Turner was All-NFL seven times and intercepted four passes in five NFL title games. Turner excelled for the Bears for 13 seasons.

On offense, Turner was a flawless snapper and an exceptional blocker who could also play guard or tackle. Never was his versatility more evident than in 1944, when he was asked to fill in as a ball carrier in an emergency situation. He consistently ground out long gains, including a 48-yard touchdown run. Three years later, against Washington, Turner came up with what he called the favorite play of his career, a 96-yard interception return for a touchdown. Turner died October 30, 1998, at the age of 79. He was a member of the 1966 Pro Football Hall of Fame class.

The Bears finished 6–3–1 in 1944, and 3–7 in 1945. The 1946 season became the final championship year of the decade, as many of the great players from 1940–41 made it back to the team following the conclusion of World War II. The Bears defeated the Giants 24–14 in New York to earn their fourth NFL championship in seven years.

Also helping to pave the way for the Bears' vaunted running game in the late 1930s and early '40s was guard Danny Fortmann. The ninth pick overall of the first NFL draft in 1936, Fortmann became the youngest starter in the NFL at the age of 20 (he was just 19 when he was drafted). A Phi Beta Kappa student at Colgate, Fortmann earned a medical degree while playing in the NFL. He was either first- or second-team All-NFL every season of his career.

A brilliant two-way performer, on offense Fortmann called signals for the linemen and was a great blocker. On defense, he was particularly adept at diagnosing offensive plays, and he was a dependable tackler. For seven seasons, Fortmann and tackle Joe Stydahar were a formidable combination on the left side of the powerful Bears line.

From 1936 to 1943, the Bears won three NFL championships and took divisional titles on two other occasions, and Fortmann was the top man at his position in the entire league. Fortmann, who graduated in 1940 from the University of Chicago Medical School, died May 23, 1995, at the age of 79.

Perhaps the Bears' best receiver during this era was Ken Kavanaugh. He had played college football at LSU, where he was named Most Valuable Player of the Southeastern Conference in 1939. Kavanaugh played for the Bears, but his career was interrupted by World War II, where he was a pilot in the European theater. He flew 30 missions and was awarded the Distinguished Flying Cross and the Air Medal with four oak leaf clusters. After the war, he continued his career with the Bears, spending a total of eight seasons in Chicago. Kavanaugh set the Bears record of 13 touchdown receptions in a season. That mark was later tied by Dick Gordon. Kavanaugh also set the mark for the highest career average gain per reception with 22.4 yards. He averaged 25.6 yards a catch in 1947.

Kavanaugh was hired by the New York Giants in 1955 as an assistant coach. He continued in that position until 1971 when he became a scout for the Giants. He retired from football in 1999. Kavanaugh, who was elected to the College Football Hall of Fame in 1963, died of complications from pneumonia on January 25, 2007, in Sarasota, Florida.

chapter 2
The Early Years

NFL legend and franchise patriarch George Halas was the foundation of the Bears for more than six decades.

Priceless Memories

For 20 years my father was a season-ticket holder to Bears home games while serving as superintendent of the Labor Relations Department at Inland Steel Company in East Chicago, Indiana. Each year, he and fellow executives would divvy up the company's allotted seats located in the East stands at Wrigley Field. Then he would come home, place the names of the seven home opponents in a hat, and my older brother and I would select three teams each that we would see that season with our father. The seventh game would go to my mother.

Not unlike the scene in Jean Shepherd's unforgettable movie *A Christmas Story*, where the father (living in Hammond, Indiana) discusses the plight of his beloved Bears while reading the paper at the kitchen table, my father displayed similar passion for his favorite NFL team.

Of course, there was no elaborate postseason scenario in the NFL in the 1950s and early '60s, only the NFL Championship Game, until the Super Bowl was instituted in 1967. I managed to go to the NFL title game in 1963 when the Bears prevailed 14–10 over the New York Giants. Wind-chill factors then were calculated by how many layers of long underwear you had to wear and, believe me, no amount was enough that frigid December day. Equipped with a mug of steaming hot chocolate, a couple of soggy ham sandwiches, a warm blanket, and a transistor radio the size of a toaster, we were good to go as WGN Radio's Jack Brickhouse and Irv Kupcinet described the action we were witnessing on the field.

Field security was pretty relaxed in those days, so my father was able to take his 8-millimeter camera and stand directly behind the visitors' bench to take footage of the teams warming up before the game.

Immediately following the games, my father and I would make a mad dash to the catwalk area underneath the stands at Wrigley Field (behind the visitors' dugout). As future Hall of Fame players such as Bobby Layne, Jim Brown, Gino Marchetti, Paul Hornung,

Lou Groza, or Johnny Unitas would stroll to their locker room in mud-stained uniforms, Bears fans would toss peanut shells and rolled-up programs at them while jeering the opposition.

A ticket for the 1963 NFL Championship Game cost $12.50. Regular-season Bears tickets went for $5. But for the good times and the memories with my father...priceless. —F.M.

Lions and Bears, Oh My!

As a child attending one of my first Bears games at Wrigley Field with my father, I quickly learned just how violent pro football can be.

The Bears entered the game with an 8–2–1 record; the Lions were 9–2. The winner of this season-finale would face the New York Giants for the NFL championship, so everything was riding on this outcome. On three different occasions, fights broke out on the field, and several times fans had to be ushered off the field under near-riot conditions.

Bobby Layne was the quarterback of the Detroit Lions in 1956 when Bears defensive end Ed Meadows delivered a vicious hit. Meadows had tackled Layne from behind after Layne had pitched out to halfback Gene Gedman. Meadows lifted Layne off his feet and buried him to the ground, sending the feisty quarterback to the locker room with a concussion. Layne's teammates were livid, claiming a late and dirty hit by Meadows.

A few plays later, Meadows was ejected for slugging Lions fullback Bill Bowman. Some say Meadows wanted to be ejected because he feared retaliation from the Lions for his hit on Layne.

But the violence wasn't over. Lions coach Buddy Parker sent defensive end Gil Mains into the game when the Bears lined up for an extra point. Quarterback Ed Brown knelt down to hold for kicker and backup quarterback George Blanda. Following instructions from his coach to retaliate against the Bears, Mains jumped on Brown's leg and then punched Blanda in the mouth. Mains was immediately ejected, but he knew he had done his job.

Fearful that Bears players would seek him out after the game, Mains had teammates surround him on the sideline as he changed out of his No. 72 jersey. The Bears won 38–21 as fans stormed out on the field before the final gun. As an eight-year-old, I thought every football game was going to be this exciting and action packed.

Mains was contacted by a writer about eight years ago and asked about the incident. He said: "Blanda still won't talk to me."

—F.M.

Jack of All Trades

The late Hall of Fame broadcaster Jack Brickhouse is best remembered for his work calling Chicago Cubs games on WGN-TV. But he also handled Bears broadcasts on WGN Radio for 24 years. His 50 years in the Chicago market alone made Brickhouse a rare eyewitness to legendary events spanning sports and politics. By the time Brickhouse retired from WGN in 1981, he had 5,300 regular-season Major League Baseball radio and television broadcasts under his belt—Cubs and Sox mostly. He also had announced Notre Dame and Big Ten football. In addition, he was the announcer of the Bulls as well as of the pro basketball teams that preceded them—the Chicago Packers and the Chicago Zephyrs. He had also broadcast pro wrestling from ringside.

"You got a dollar's worth of entertainment for your dollar, and I defy football, baseball, or any of the rest of them to match that," he said, defending pro wrestling.

Brickhouse also covered five national political conventions, Franklin Roosevelt's 1945 inauguration, and the parade welcoming General Douglas McArthur to Chicago. He reported from an airplane circling the city checking blackout procedures during WWII, from the streets of Paris and Bangkok as part of a worldwide report on foreign attitudes toward America, and from atop a 254-foot broadcast tower in Peoria, Illinois.

Someone figured out no man in history had broadcast more losing games.

I once asked Jack how he managed to remain so upbeat while broadcasting so many losing Bears seasons in the 1950s and 1970s. The worst season ever was 1969 when the Bears finished 1–13, despite having future Hall of Famers Dick Butkus and Gale Sayers on that roster. Brickhouse noted that Sayers had suffered a devastating knee injury in 1968, but returned in 1969 following an arduous rehab program. Sayers managed to gain over 1,000 yards to lead the league in rushing on that 1–13 team. Brickhouse remembered that Sayers's longest run that season was only 28 yards, but he sort of reinvented himself by running more between the tackles.

The last time the Arizona Cardinals won an NFL title was 1947, when they were the Chicago Cardinals. Guess who was behind the microphone for their games?

That's right, Jack Brickhouse. —F.M.

Field of Dreams

Many of the former Bears who played their home games at Wrigley Field were not thrilled when the team moved to Soldier Field.

"Wrigley Field was really unique," former Bears center Mike Pyle said. He was a captain on the 1963 NFL championship team. "If you remember, one corner of the end zone was over the first-base dugout, and I can remember vividly [Bears defensive back] Roosevelt Taylor flying into the American Legion band tuba. There was a special aura for the Bears because the fans were so close. The new stadiums have so much more space for TV production and expensive seats. I was never a great fan of Soldier Field because of the distance from the field."

Pyle played nine seasons with the Bears after graduating from Yale, and he participated in the 1964 Pro Bowl.

Gale Sayers said he used to love playing football in Wrigley Field, even though that was the site of his devastating knee injury in 1968 suffered when Kermit Alexander of the 49ers tackled him.

The NFL made the Bears move out of Wrigley Field after half a century of playing there because it did not hold the minimum of 50,000 fans.

Bleachers were added at Wrigley to increase capacity and put more fans closer to the action, and eventually the Bears organization acquired a large, portable bleacher section that spanned the right- and center-field areas. This East Stand raised Wrigley's football capacity to about 46,000—still 4,000 shy of the requirement. After the Bears left, those East bleachers were transported to Soldier Field as the North Stand, until they were replaced by permanent seating.

Besides the issue of fan capacity, Wrigley was hardly a perfect venue for football. The Bears players dressed in the same locker room that the Chicago Cubs used, which was in the left-field corner of the stadium. Those were tight quarters for 45 football players, a coaching staff, and team trainers. There were four or five showers in that whole locker room for the entire group, and half the time the water was cold.

In addition, like many NFL fields that were shared with baseball teams back then, the sod that covered the infield would become undone during games, especially when it was cold.

The football field ran north to south, from left field to the foul side of first base. The remodeling of the bleachers made it an even tighter fit. As a matter of fact, the corner of the south end zone was in the visiting baseball team's dugout, which was filled with pads for safety. That required a special ground rule that sliced off that corner of the end zone. One corner of the north end line ran just inches short of the left-field wall.

There is a legend described in the Pro Football Hall of Fame archives that Bronko Nagurski, the Hall of Fame Bears fullback, once bulldozed his way through the defense and then ran all the way through that end zone before slamming his head on the bricks. And they wore leather helmets back then.

Nagurski supposedly went back to the bench and told Coach Halas, "That last guy gave me quite a lick!" That incident must

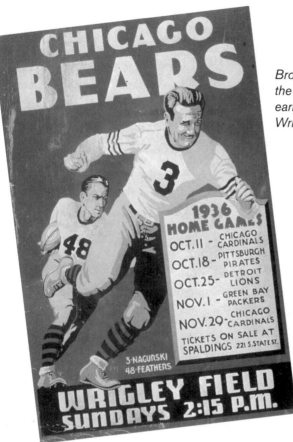

Bronko Nagurski and the Bears played their early home games at Wrigley Field.

have been why the Bears decided to put some padding in front of that wall.

But Wrigley Field retains some cherished memories for many longtime Bears fans. The Bears are second only to the Green Bay Packers in total NFL championships, and all but one of those came during their tenure at Wrigley. The Bears called Soldier Field home the year they captured Super Bowl XX. The Bears had one experimental game at Dyche Stadium on the Northwestern University campus in Evanston, Illinois, but otherwise continued at Wrigley until transferring to Soldier Field on the lakefront. —F.M.

Roger and Out

The College All-Star Game used to be held at Soldier Field in Chicago. Each year, the top college seniors would face the defending NFL champion. It was sort of a kickoff to the football season, and huge crowds would attend.

The first College All-Star Game was held in 1934, the brain-child of sports editor Arch Ward of the *Chicago Tribune*. The game was played annually through 1976, and raised something like $4 million for Chicago charities. Most of the games were played at Soldier Field, but two were played at Northwestern University. An NFL players' strike in 1974 caused the cancellation of the game that year.

The last College All-Star Game was played in 1976 against the Pittsburgh Steelers. The Super Bowl X champions were leading 24–0 when lightning and thunderstorms descended, making conditions unsafe for players and fans. Rowdy fans tore down the goal posts after players were ordered to leave the field. After the game was called, Chicago Tribune Charities chose not to resume the contests in 1977. The series ended with the NFL champions winning 31 games and the College All-Stars nine. There were two ties.

Cooper Rollow, sports editor of the *Chicago Tribune* at the time and president of Chicago Tribune Charities, Inc., said the quick cancellation in 1976 came "because of the weather, danger-ous field conditions, and the risk to injury for players and fans."

On December 22, 1976, Robert M. Hunt of Chicago Tribune Charities announced: "We regret the end of a traditional sports classic which has contributed substantial assistance to the needy in Chicagoland. Unfortunately, problems which make con-tinuation impossible have been created by uncertainties in recruiting player personnel and increasing expenses reflected in insurance costs that doubled last year alone because of high player salaries."

Hall of Fame quarterback Roger Staubach has talked about how important the 1965 College All-Star Game was to his burgeoning

NFL career. NFL scouts realized that he was more than just a good college player.

"I think those couple of weeks working out there convinced Dallas and Kansas City to draft me in case I would ever leave the service," said Staubach. "It turned out great. We lost to the Browns in that All-Star Game 21–17. I hurt my left shoulder in that game when Galen Fiss hit me in the second quarter. But in those couple of weeks the scouts saw I could be an NFL quarterback." —F.M.

On the Defensive

When the discussion turns to the best defenses in NFL history, the 1985 Bears immediately pop into the discussion, and for good reason. But the 1963 NFL champion Bears featured an imposing defense as well. Hall of Fame defensive end Doug Atkins always reminds me that the '63 Bears allowed only about 10 points a game, and it often was incumbent upon the defense to provide winning plays. As a youngster, I attended the '63 championship game with my father at Wrigley Field. On that frigid, single-digit temperature afternoon, the Bears defense scored one touchdown and set up the other one in a 14–10 triumph.

Atkins was a 6'8", 285-pound defender with tremendous athletic ability. He high-jumped six feet, eight inches when he was at the University of Tennessee. And as a member of the Bears, he often high-jumped over would-be blockers en route to sacking the quarterback.

Other key members of that Bears defense included fellow Hall of Famers Bill George and Stan Jones, as well as Larry Morris, Joe Fortunato, Ed O'Bradovich, Rosey Taylor, and Richie Petitbon. Atkins also was known as a rebellious free spirit. As part of the initiation and hazing of rookies back then, Atkins and other veterans would take the first-year players out and get them drunk with his patented, 110-proof Fighting Cock whiskey.

Atkins played 17 seasons in the NFL, 12 with the Bears, after being selected in the first round out of Tennessee by the

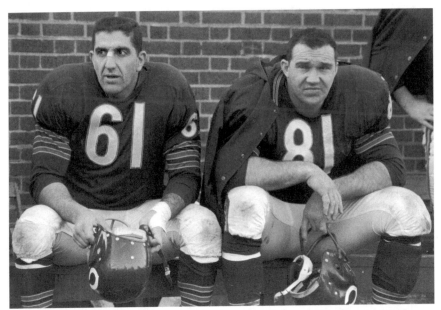

Bill George (left) and Doug Atkins were anchors on the Bears' 1963 championship defense.

Cleveland Browns. The eight-time Pro Bowl selection played in an era when head slaps and late hits on the quarterback were not subject to review, scrutiny, or penalty.

"If I used a head slap, it wasn't intentional," Atkins said. "In the old days, it didn't matter where you hit 'em. They have softened the game up. And I don't think the officials are as good as they used to be."

So, which defense was better? The '85 Bears or the '63 Bears?

"I think we might have beat [the '85 Bears] by a point or two," said Atkins, who feels the NFL game has changed significantly since he played. "It looks like a bunch of Sumo wrestlers at the line of scrimmage nowadays. They get engaged in their blocks and they are all hugging and stuff. I don't know why they can't use a head slap anymore." —F.M.

Defense Wins Championships

What is it about defensive coordinators and the special place they occupy in the hearts of successful Bears teams? At the conclusion of Super Bowl XX, Bears players hoisted defensive coordinator Buddy Ryan onto their shoulders, as well as head coach Mike Ditka. Way back in 1963, George Allen was given a game ball after he masterminded a defense that prevailed over the New York Giants in the NFL Championship Game.

Allen, who passed away in 1990 at the age of 72, served as the head coach of the Los Angeles Rams from 1966 to 1970 and for the Washington Redskins from 1971 to 1977. He had a regular-season record of 116–47–5 and never had a losing season in 12 years as an NFL head coach.

"My father left each kid a different symbol. He didn't want to leave us any money or anything like that. This is his 1963 Bears championship ring," one of his sons, Bruce Allen, said. "Inside the ring it says: '5 interceptions, 2 fumbles.' To him, the joy of winning is special. I never saw him feel that an individual accomplishment meant as much as a team accomplishment. So I think his Hall of Fame honor is for all the coaches and staff that worked with him."

Allen was well respected by former Bears head coach and NFL pioneer George Halas, who presented him with the game ball after the 14–10 NFL championship victory. "I know that to my dad the name *George Halas* means about everything," said Allen. —F.M.

chapter 3

Gale, Butkus, and Papa Bear

Dick Butkus became the prototype NFL linebacker during his nine-year career with the Bears.

Rosey Outlook

It did not take very long for Gale Sayers to make an indelible impression in the NFL. During his first season, Sayers scored an NFL rookie record 22 touchdowns, including six in one game against the San Francisco 49ers.

In the Bears' 1965 home opener against the Rams, Sayers introduced himself to stellar 300-pound defensive lineman Rosey Grier. Sayers gained just 12 yards on nine carries that game, but he managed to catch a screen pass and maneuver 80 yards for a touchdown. After that game, Grier was asked by reporters about the Bears' rookie sensation.

"I hit him so hard, I thought my shoulder must have busted him in two," said Grier. "I heard a roar from the crowd and figured he had fumbled, so I started scrambling around looking for the loose ball. But there was no ball and Sayers was gone."

And, by the way, the Bears won that game 31–6 as Sayers also threw an option pass to Dick Gordon for a 26-yard touchdown. In 1977, Sayers became the youngest man ever inducted into the Pro Football Hall of Fame at the tender age of 34. —F.M.

Pushing the Right Buttons

Dick Butkus earned his reputation as one of the toughest men ever to play in the NFL. The Hall of Fame middle linebacker was quiet and shy off the field, but he was a one-man wrecking crew on it. And, it seemed, it didn't take much to get him angry enough to want to rip the head off the opposing quarterback.

George Halas knew how to push the button that would get Butkus foaming at the mouth before a game. Butkus always had a strong desire to play well against the Detroit Lions. Early in his career, Butkus was practicing his long snaps before a game against the Lions when Halas strolled over to him and said, "Hey, did you hear what Flanagan said about you?"

Ed Flanagan was the Lions' center.

Gale Sayers posted a Hall of Fame career in just 68 remarkable games.

Butkus said to Halas, "No, what did he say?"

At that point, Halas just walked away. He simply wanted to start a rivalry between the two men.

Butkus appreciates Halas's pioneering effort to start a new professional league, handling the business end as well as the coaching. Even though Butkus ended his career with the Bears haggling over a medical treatment dispute, he will forever hold Halas in the highest regard.

"Everybody would talk about how cheap he was, but later on you would find out about all the people he would really help," Butkus said. "He never let it be known. I think he was great for the game, great for the league. And having been from Chicago myself and playing for the founder of football, it was neat. He was a no b.s. guy. That's the way I was brought up. And I think we hit it off great. One minute he would be yelling at you and the next minute he would be patting you on the back." —F.M.

Oh, What a Relief!

A few years ago I had the opportunity to witness the unveiling of a dramatic 26½-foot-tall granite bas-relief sculpture, depicting a time line describing George Halas's contribution to professional football and the history of the Bears. The impressive sight was unveiled in Soldier Field's Bear Den, located in the west concourse.

I caught up with Bears Hall of Fame linebacker Dick Butkus at the ceremony. "It's right on the mark. It looks like he is yelling at people. That's what he did," Butkus said of the eight-foot-high laser-etched image of Papa Bear. "They got him down good."

Then I came across Hall of Fame running back Gale Sayers and asked for his reaction. "Coach Halas was a great friend and a great mentor of mine. It is always good to hear something good about him," he said. "A lot of times, when I was playing, there was a lot of bad written about George Halas. But he founded the National Football League and made it what it is today. If it weren't for George Halas and the people who are up there on this [sculpture], there wouldn't be an NFL today. The lady [artist, Julie Rotblatt-Amrany] did a great job on it and I am happy to be up on it. Because my career wasn't that long. It was 68 ballgames. Most of these [other] players played 10 or 12 years."

Family members of the remaining six Bears legends highlighted on the 11,500-pound memorial also were in attendance, representing Walter Payton, Mike Singletary, Bill George, Sid Luckman, Red Grange, and Bronko Nagurski.

Michael McCaskey, Bears chairman of the board and grandson of Halas, pointed out, "[Halas] was the son of Czech immigrants, born on the north side of Chicago. He helped found the

Dick Butkus is one of the most beloved Bears of all time.

National Football League and the Bears. He had Chicago woven through the fabric of his life."

Virginia McCaskey, Halas's daughter, also attended the ceremony along with several other members of the McCaskey family. Michael McCaskey explained that Halas grew up a Cubs fan and therefore reasoned that the name of Chicago's pro football franchise naturally should be the Bears. A University of Illinois alumnus with a degree in engineering, Halas then borrowed the colors of the Fighting Illini for his charter franchise.

Sayers recalled meeting Halas for the first time after being a quiet and shy first-round draft pick out of Kansas in 1965. "You respect older people and that is the way I was brought up," said Sayers. "I never had a problem with George Halas. All he wanted you to do was to show up in shape and give 100 percent. And I did that. A lot of players wouldn't come to training camp in shape. And three weeks into camp, we had our first exhibition game. You can't get in shape in three weeks."

Sayers tied an NFL record by scoring six touchdowns in one muddy game against the San Francisco 49ers at Wrigley Field in 1965. His six TDs included an 80-yard pass reception, a 50-yard rush, and an 85-yard punt return. But Halas was not prone to heaping individual praise on his ballplayers.

"He didn't say anything unusual," said Sayers. "Back then, we weren't interested in records and anything like that. If you got ahead by 20 points, you took out the first string and put in the second string. I probably could have scored eight touchdowns that particular day. It didn't make any difference, and we wanted to win the ballgame. After that game, he [Halas] said, 'You had a great game.' And that was it. That's all I wanted to hear. We went about our business and things worked out."

One former Bears Hall of Famer whose likeness was not on the sculpture was Mike Ditka, whose feud with the McCaskey family remained at full tilt. —F.M.

Toilet Humor

Abe Gibron was the Bears head coach in the early 1970s and is remembered for his, shall we say, *informal* way of dealing with people. The media covering the Bears at that time basically included just the beat reporters from the three major newspapers.

It was nothing like the hordes of radio, television, newspaper, and Internet reporters who show up at Halas Hall these days. Following one particular practice session, Gibron was going over the events of the day with the reporters. At one point, Gibron excused himself to go to the bathroom. He left the bathroom door ajar so that he could continue his conversation with the writers!

Gibron was a likeable character, for sure, but his three-year record with the Bears was just 11–30–1.

Former Bears linebacker Doug Buffone played under five head coaches during his career in Chicago, including Gibron. Buffone recalls that Gibron used to host cookouts every Wednesday night when the team trained in Rensselaer, Indiana. Gibron, who weighed nearly 400 pounds and loved to eat, would announce to the players: "It's Wednesday night, guys! This is it. Everybody out into the woods." The players would build a bonfire and bring a couple of kegs of beer. Some players would bring a couple of lambs to roast on a spit. Some players swear they saw Gibron polish off 20 ears of corn in one sitting as the team enjoyed the festivities until 11:00 at night.

Not only was Gibron popular with his players and the fans, but he also seemed to know everyone in town who had a connection to scrumptious food. Gibron was an outstanding offensive guard with the Cleveland Browns, but food was the highlight for him during his days as an NFL head coach. —F.M.

A Real Battler

Over the years I have had a chance to know former Bears quarterback Bobby Douglass, even though he had moved on from the Bears by the time I joined the team. Douglass was a second-round draft pick out of Kansas who was known for his hard-throwing left arm and his ability to run with the football. In fact, he held the record for most rushing yards by an NFL quarterback for 34 years. He rushed for 968 yards in a 14-game schedule in 1972. Michael Vick broke the mark with 1,039 yards in 2006, although it took him

16 games. Douglass also played for the Chargers, the Saints, and the Packers. He retired after the 1978 season, his 10ᵗʰ season playing in the NFL. I was troubled to learn that the once-strapping 6'3", 225-pound Douglass had lost 50 pounds because of a bout with cancer in 2007.

Douglass attended Super Bowl XLI in Miami to watch the Bears face the Indianapolis Colts. On his way home he noticed a little swelling in his neck. He went to the doctor and was diagnosed with squamous-cell cancer. Douglass described the health scare this way: "The hardest thing I have had to do, certainly. You just are not 100 percent yourself. I am tired at times. I have an equilibrium problem right now because of one of the medications I am on. It's a tough fight, but I have to thank God that they think

For 34 years, Bobby Douglass held the record for most rushing yards by a quarterback in a single season.

I am cancer free. I will beat this and regain those 50 pounds, believe me."

After several months of treatment and rehabilitation, he was doing much better. He had regained 30 pounds by Christmas 2007. And I certainly hope and pray he pulls through this crisis. Douglass was a raw talent during his playing days who probably never reached his potential. Part of that probably had to do with the fact that he had four different head coaches with the Bears— George Halas, Jim Dooley, Abe Gibron, and Jack Pardee. Then Douglass had a new offensive coordinator practically each year. Zeke Bratkowski was the only coordinator he had two years in a row.

As a passer, he completed just 507 of 1,178 attempts for 36 touchdowns and 64 interceptions with a quarterback passer rating of only 48.5 during his career. Douglass didn't have that buffer to help him navigate through the tough transition into the NFL. —D.J.

Wally's World

I will never forget how badly Wally Chambers wanted to be traded away from the Bears between the 1977 and 1978 seasons. The Bears wanted Tampa Bay's number one draft pick for Wally, and Wally suggested that I go along with him in the deal. Now, Tampa Bay was an expansion team at that time and hadn't won a game the first couple of years, so I wasn't too anxious to go down there. As it turned out, the Bears would eventually deal Chambers to the Bucs for their number one pick, which they used to take Dan Hampton out of Arkansas.

Chambers had issues dealing with our coach at the time, Jack Pardee. Pardee came in and was trying to change the culture that existed on the Bears under former coach Abe Gibron. One time, Pardee claimed he overheard Chambers and Lionel Antoine saying they were planning to skip out on the afternoon portion of the two-a-day practices in Lake Forest. Pardee later confronted

Chambers and Antoine in front of a team meeting. But each player boldly stood up and denied saying what Pardee was convinced he overheard.

Pardee would take the Bears to the playoffs in 1977, but he left the club shortly afterward to take the head coaching position with the Washington Redskins. —D.J.

Purple People Eaters

Carl Eller's next-to-last year as a full-time player in the NFL was my rookie season of 1976. Lucky for me. Eller, the Hall of Fame defensive end, was one of the famed Minnesota Vikings "Purple People Eaters" that included Jim Marshall at the opposite end, and Hall of Famers Alan Page and Gary Larsen at the tackles.

Eller, whose career with the Vikings spanned from 1964 to 1978, did not play his home games in the Metrodome, but in the outdoor Metropolitan Stadium in Bloomington, Minnesota. He recalls playing against both Gale Sayers and Walter Payton, and those star running backs had some of their greatest games against the Vikings. Eller called Sayers and Payton "some of the real classic heroes of the game. It was very difficult to defend them.

"The thing about our games with the Bears, we never had an advantage on those guys, no matter what the record was," he continued. "It was always a tough game, whether it was a home game or down at Soldier Field. We had a lot of respect for the Bears, even at the times when we probably shouldn't have."

Eller remembers the classic Bears-Vikings battles in the 1960s and '70s during a period in which he won the George Halas Award in 1971 as the NFL's leading defensive player and was selected to play in six Pro Bowls (1969–72, 1974, and 1975).

"The one thing about the Central Division back when we played, everybody played in the same kind of climate," said Eller. "They all had outdoor stadiums—Detroit, Green Bay, and of course, the Bears. It was like we were cold-weather guys. And one of the coldest games I can remember was against the Bears at Metropolitan Stadium." —D.J.

All in the Family

Like it or not, Tom Waddle may have heard all of the stories about the early years of pro football while sitting around the Thanksgiving table with family. That's because the father-in-law of the former Bears receiver is Gino Cappelletti. Cappelletti starred as a receiver and place-kicker for the old Boston Patriots of the American Football League. In 1964, he was named the AFL's Player of the Year when he scored 155 points by catching seven touchdown passes, kicking 25 field goals and 36 extra points, and cashing in a two-point conversion.

Cappelletti has been doing color commentary for the New England Patriots on WBCN radio since 1972. And Waddle has fashioned a very impressive sports broadcasting career of his own in Chicago since his playing days concluded. Cappelletti spent 11 seasons with the team (1960–70) as one of the original members of the franchise. He is one of only three players to play in every game in the AFL's history. He led the AFL in scoring five times when the Patriots played their home games on rough, archaic natural surfaces.

"Of course, things were different back in the '60s," he said. "Of the eight teams in the American Football League then, six of them played on baseball fields, because they shared their stadiums with the baseball teams in the respective cities.

"There were only two teams that had strictly football stadiums, and that was the San Diego Chargers at Balboa Stadium and Houston at Jeppesen Stadium. So we had to make adjustments and we had to use some strategy because of the fields. Sometimes you would be on the infield sand, because they never filled them in with grass in those days. And it made for a little difficulty when it came to place-kicking."

Cappelletti, who ranks second on the Patriots' all-time scoring list with 1,130 points (42 touchdowns, 176 field goals, 342 extra points, and four two-point conversions), often spends Thanksgiving in Chicago with his daughter, his son-in-law, and his four granddaughters. Asked if Waddle had heard the stories of his hardships as one of the game's pioneers, Cappelletti smiled and said, "Tom will take out a hankie and wipe out a tear now and then. The only way today's players can appreciate what we pro football pioneers went through is if you experienced it." —F.M.

Here Comes the Judge

We used to call Bob Thomas "Money" when he came through with winning kicks for the Bears in the 1970s. Now maybe I should be calling him for a loan. As the Illinois Supreme Court Chief Justice, Thomas won a $7 million libel suit against a suburban Chicago newspaper. The legal battle involved two columns that were critical of Thomas published by the *Kane County Chronicle*. In 2003, Bill Page's columns accused Thomas of meddling in the disciplinary case of former Kane County state's attorney Meg Gorecki, who was caught on tape suggesting that a friend could obtain a county job by donating to another county official.

"It was very emotional," said Thomas, who cried and hugged his attorneys after Judge Donald O'Brien read the verdict. "When the judge said the verdict went in favor of the plaintiff, I just broke down. You realize how much your reputation and integrity mean to you. I try my best to live with integrity, and to have that attacked and then have 12 jurors say, 'You've got your reputation back,' there were a lot of tears. I believe about nine or 10 of [the jurors] hugged me on the way out the door. They were crying and I was crying. And they said, 'Hold your head high.' I have never been on that side of the bench before. It was eye opening. But I do thank God and I thank my attorneys and I thank those 12 jurors for resoundingly saying that my integrity was attacked and there was no truth to those frivolous allegations."

Thomas was represented in the case by Chicago attorney Joseph A. Power of Power Rogers & Smith, PC. Power had successfully represented former Bears players Tony Blaylock and Ron Morris, as well as the team's longtime strength coach Clyde Emrich, in previous unrelated legal matters.

I cannot help but recall Bob's shining hour at Giants Stadium in 1977. His overtime field goal in the final game of the regular season put us in the playoffs for the first time in 14 years. A Notre Dame alumnus, Thomas shares the Bears record for the longest field goal—55 yards—with Kevin Butler. Thomas kicked for us from 1975 to 1984. —D.J.

The Living End

One of the Bears' all-time great wide receivers has suffered more injuries since he retired from the NFL. Harlon Hill, age 75, was the NFL's Rookie of the Year in 1954, catching 45 passes for 1,124 yards and 12 touchdowns during a 12-game season. He averaged 25 yards a reception in his inaugural year.

In 1955, he was the league's Most Valuable Player. Not bad for a 15th-round draft pick from obscure Florence State Teachers College in Alabama. The school is now known as the University of North Alabama. Sadly, in 2007, the former Bears three-time Pro Bowl receiver suffered from a variety of injuries, including two broken hips, five broken ribs, three aneurysms, excruciating arthritis pain, and he underwent brain surgery on Valentine's Day. Hill's four daughters—Gwen, Jackie, Janet, and Teresa—were taking turns watching their dad, who is barely mobile with a walker. His wife, Virginia, also is in poor health. Hill's son, Jerry, is now the head football coach at the high school where Harlon served as principal when he retired.

Hill wishes the rules of the game when he played were the way they are now when it comes to the contact between wide receivers and defensive backs. At 6'3", 195 pounds when he played, Hill took a beating going over the middle and on down-and-out patterns in the 1950s.

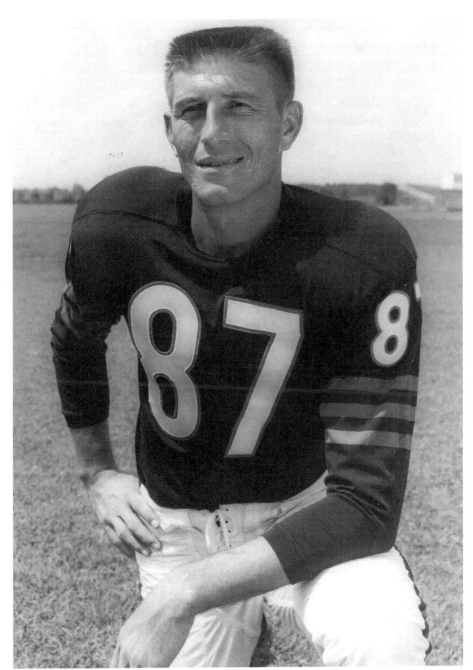

Receiver Harlon Hill was the NFL's Rookie of the Year in 1954.

"The receivers nowadays look like they are playing touch football," Hill told me. "The refs won't let the defensive backs touch them past five yards. The receivers can run where they want to down the field. That's the biggest difference."

The Harlon Hill Trophy has been awarded annually since 1986 to the NCAA Division II college football player of the year. Hill was named an NAIA All-American in his senior year of 1953. —F.M.

chapter 4
Greetings from Platteville!

Walter Payton and William Perry share a scooter in Platteville, Wisconsin.
(Photo courtesy of Bill Smith)

Mice and Men

When I played for the Bears, we trained during the summer at Lake Forest College in a suburb north of Chicago. One of the strangest things we would notice each day was that part of the leather inserts in our helmets seemed to be missing. Little chunks were taken out. It was soon determined that mice had infiltrated our lockers, lured by the smell of moist and salty sweat on the leather inside the helmets, and had been nibbling away. Yuck!

Every training camp seems to have its special set of unusual memories. The University of Wisconsin–Platteville, located 180 miles northwest of Chicago, began hosting the Bears in 1984. Before Platteville, we trained at Lake Forest College (1975–83). Before that, it was St. Joseph's College in Rensselaer, Indiana (1944–74), St. John's Military Academy in Delafield, Wisconsin (1935–43), Lane Tech High School (1934), and the University of Notre Dame in South Bend, Indiana (1933).

Hall of Fame Bears defensive end Doug Atkins remembers training camp in Rensselaer, when players would break curfew late at night. Assistant coaches and trainers would place their hand on the engines of players' cars in the parking lot to see if they were warm. That way they could determine if guys were sneaking out after bed check.

Former Bears safety Dave Duerson remembers how Platteville grew on him. He said he will always remember Platteville for being a cow town with cornfields and 100-degree weather. He remembers the thousands of people showing up to watch the Bears practice. But by the time Duerson's career was over with the Bears in 1989, Platteville had become a bustling community with a bunch of hotels sitting where cornfields used to stand. —D.J.

Platteville Pranks

As memory serves me, it was a hot, sticky night in Platteville in 1984 and Walter Payton was bored, restless, and searching for

Defensive end Dan Hampton was a gentle giant when it came to interacting with the fans. (Photo courtesy of Bill Smith)

a way to entertain himself and his Chicago Bears teammates during training camp. So he tossed a lighted firecracker inside the dormitory—at 4:00 in the morning!

Walter was known for more than stiff-arming would-be tacklers and churning his muscular legs for record-setting yardage. We all knew him as the ultimate prankster, the guy you had better keep an eye on, lest you become his next victim. Steve Zielke, who retired in 2007 as assistant chancellor for business affairs at UW–Platteville, was a firsthand witness to many of Payton's antics. "There were Walter's firecrackers going off all of the time," he recalled. "They would go off at 2:00 in the morning or 4:00 in the morning. If he had to get up in the middle of the night or something, he would throw a firecracker out."

I will always remember Walter's kindness with the kids. He would often play catch with a kid in the crowd when he wasn't doing something in practice. And he would stay after practice and sign autographs for anyone who asked.

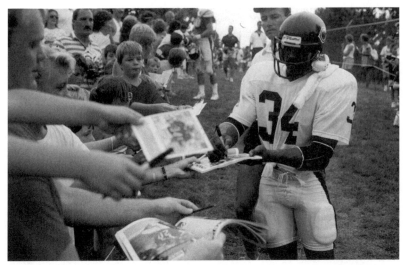

Walter Payton takes time out from practice to sign autographs during Bears training camp. (Photo courtesy of Bill Smith)

There were a lot of other characters on the team, too. Kurt Becker (1982–88, 1990) was always pulling pranks on somebody, whether it was the ball boys or other players. Those were really great times.

The 18-year relationship between the Bears and this previously inconspicuous town of about 10,000 people reached amicable closure in 2002. The memories and amusing anecdotes associated with the longtime Bears summer training site will never die. In fact, they will undoubtedly become grossly embellished over the course of time. The Bears relocated to Olivet Nazarene University in Bourbonnais, Illinois, in 2003. —F.M.

No Fear

The people of Platteville initially embraced the Bears with a fair amount of trepidation. Ditka's reputation as a demanding, short-tempered coach preceded him. The university's main worry was the behavior of the players as well as some of the coaches because of their public images at the time. The folks in Platteville worried about what the players were going to be like, how much trouble they were going to have, who was going to be in jail...all of that kind of stuff. But there really wasn't much of that. It was a wonderful surprise for them.

Steve Zielke, who worked for UW–Platteville, said his biggest concern when the Bears first decided to come to Platteville was Ditka, because of how he was portrayed. And yet he turned out to be the kindest and most generous person they probably ever had on campus.

Those mean old growling Bears, as they had been portrayed, were in many ways just normal human beings. There were no major problems in all of their years at the university. The only physical damage was to a mirror in the hallway of a dormitory when a couple of rookies were goofing off wrestling. Most other NFL camps have not had that kind of luck.

The dwindling crowds watching the Bears train in Platteville in the early 2000s was a reflection of the team's failure to churn out a winner. The year after the Super Bowl, 1986, there were more than 80,000 people in Platteville during a 34-day period. There were average crowds in those years of 2,000 to 3,000 for practices. When the New Orleans Saints came in to scrimmage the Bears, there were about 8,500 people a day in Platteville. But in the final years in Platteville, the crowds dwindled to about 200 on the weekdays and probably 1,000 or 1,200 on the weekends.

The Platteville community was bracing for a significant financial hit because of the Bears' decision to leave their facility. And the Bears regenerated the financial and emotional support for their team at the new training site at Olivet Nazarene. —F.M.

Lost Time

Walter was one of the biggest pranksters on the Bears team. In the early years when the Bears were in Platteville, the players seemed a lot more fun-loving. After the salaries of the players went up so high, things became a lot more serious around campus. They worked a little harder in a more disciplined fashion and there wasn't as much mischief anymore.

But I recall one Platteville incident in 1984 involving Payton and his close friend and teammate Matt Suhey that nearly cost Platteville the honor of hosting the Bears. It's a funny story that wasn't so funny at the time. Suhey had a nice Rolex watch with diamonds on it and everything. Matt was in Walter's trailer and happened to leave it there. So Walter thought he would hide it for a week. Matt was very concerned that someone had stolen his watch. In that five-day period before Walter gave the watch back, Steve Zielke interviewed probably 100 people who could have had access to it. That's all he did for five days. He couldn't sleep at night. Zielke was wondering who could have done this. Then, at the end of the week, Walter came up to Suhey and said innocently, "Matt, did you lose this watch?" Zielke could have clobbered Walter.

Kathy Kopp, head of the Platteville Chamber of Commerce, has tried to keep the memory of the Bears alive by implementing a special room dedicated to Bears memorabilia from those previous 18 years. She said the way she was looking at the situation was very bittersweet. They were so proud to host the Bears camp every year, and they were thankful for the attention that it brought to the Platteville community and their local university. The fans were fantastic and there were a number of them who were on a first-name basis with the players who came up there every year. Chicagoans really enjoyed the small-town atmosphere and the laid-back quality of life. —F.M.

Picking Up the Tab

It was dinnertime at training camp in Platteville, Wisconsin, in 1989. I was the beat writer covering the Bears for the *Chicago Tribune*, and my counterpart with the *Chicago Sun-Times* was Dan Pompei. We decided to head over to a restaurant called the Timbers Supper Club to grab a bite to eat.

The restaurant was a little busy at the time, so we were asked to sit at the bar until our table was ready. We ordered a couple of drinks and sat there with a couple of radio guys from Chicago and began shooting the breeze. As we grabbed our drinks, a voice at the other end of the bar barked out: "Put 'em on my tab." Sure enough, it was Mike Ditka.

We thanked him for the drinks and dared to engage Ditka in some small talk away from our usually confrontational press conference setting. The give-and-take conversation was quite pleasant. For once, we had a chance to talk to Ditka about our lives and backgrounds. I told him about our similarities of growing up in steel mill towns. I grew up in Gary, Indiana, and Ditka in Aliquippa, Pennsylvania. I told him I had been a high school football and track coach in Grove City, Ohio, after playing football and running track in college.

Everything was off the record and low-key. When the waitress told us our table was ready, we decided to eat our dinner at the bar so that we could continue our lighthearted discussion. Ditka shared his memories of George Halas and his family experiences growing up in Pennsylvania. He seemed genuine and relaxed. It was a totally pleasant and unexpected experience. —F.M.

Really Big Men on Campus

Rowdy Bears players invading the Platteville bars during the height of the Mike Ditka era fortunately never crossed the line from mischievous to criminal behavior, although I remember some close calls. Platteville Police Chief Earl Hernandez, who retired from the Illinois State Police force after 30 years to become head of the Platteville force, made sure we didn't lose our heads.

According to Hernandez, the Platteville police never had any problems with the Bears players or staff. The police did, however, have a few problems with fans who had a tendency to get a little rambunctious in the bar district. The Platteville police usually staffed one more officer while the Bears were in town, only because of the number of people who were there. But from the Bears' perspective, there was really no problem with them. The college students gave the police far more problems during the school year than the Bears did.

Local merchants over the years placed pictures of Bears players in their storefronts as part of an "Adopt a Bear" program. The Bears players seemed to become part of the community during the summer. Everybody just accepted them, even though Platteville is considered a Packers town. There might have been 10 or 20 Bears fans who lived there then. But when the Bears were there for those four to six weeks, the place became a Bears town.

Dorian Smith took over as owner of the popular Hoist House in downtown Platteville two years before the Bears left. The Hoist House was built in the 1890s as a bar. Smith said he felt they were going to miss out on some business. But more than that, he missed out on seeing the fans and the media and Bears person-nel. He said those were the people he really had fun with. Luckily, he had the college season to fall back on. Other popular restau-rants and nightspots in Platteville included Pizzeria Uno, Donisi's, Gadzooks, and the Patio Lounge. —F.M.

William "The Refrigerator" Perry was often the center of attention during training camp. (Photo courtesy of Bill Smith)

Wheels of Fortune

During the Ditka era, it was not uncommon for players such as Jay Hilgenberg and Tom Thayer to make the 180-mile trek from Chicago to Platteville on motorcycles. Once on the UW–Platteville campus, many players got around on scooters.

In 1987, tackle Keith Van Horne decided to really put his scooter's pedal to the metal and he ended up injuring his toe. That put him out of action for quite a while. That same year, Jim Harbaugh was riding one of those scooters when a guy opened his car door and Harbaugh slammed into it. The car door was ruined, and more significantly, Harbaugh missed about a week of practice with an injury. The following year, Ditka put his foot down by saying the players could not ride scooters around training camp any longer.

Harbaugh, for one, came from a very disciplined background. His father, Jack, was a longtime football coach at the high school

Jim McMahon leads a pack of scooters in Platteville, Wisconsin.
(Photo courtesy of Bill Smith)

and college level. In fact, Jim is currently the head coach at Stanford where his late father once coached.

All Bears fans remember when Mike Ditka got in the face of Harbaugh and chewed him out. Now it is time for Harbaugh to do the yelling at his players.

"Only when they screw up," he insists. "Actually, I am really hands-on. It is a game played by emotional people and I am an emotional guy. I coach aggressively because I want them to play aggressively. I guess I yell a lot. But I always try to yell something positive with the kids."

Harbaugh says he tries to take something from all of the coaches he had as a player. "Probably a combination of my dad, Bo Schembechler, Mike Ditka, Lindy Infante, Ted Marchibroda, Mike Riley, Ron Turner.... I have taken so much from each one of those guys," he said.

His first seven NFL seasons were with the Bears, where he passed for a career-high 3,121 yards in 1991. "I remember most just playing for a team with a great tradition, more than anything," he said. "I cherish the relationships I made with guys on the team, coaches there, and people in the city. There is just something about the pride of being a Chicago Bear. That is something that will stay with me forever, for as long as I live."

In 1995 with the Colts, Harbaugh achieved career highs in completion percentage (63.7) and touchdown passes (17). He led the Colts to the AFC Championship Game before being voted to the Pro Bowl and being named Comeback Player of the Year. The Colts' offense seemed better suited to his talents. "Lindy Infante, just from a technical standpoint in football, was great. Having Marshall Faulk was big. Sometimes for a quarterback, it is a function of who else is on the team," he said. —D.J.

Three Not of a Kind

Over a period of three decades of covering the Bears, I had the opportunity to know three head coaches pretty well: Ditka, Dave

Wannstedt, and Dick Jauron. Ditka spent many evenings enjoying a cold one at the VFW Hall in downtown Platteville or at the Timbers Restaurant during training camp.

Wannstedt once hosted a dinner session for us in the media at a restaurant called Rebels in nearby Belmont, Wisconsin. Sportswriters were greeted by a velvet portrait of Elvis Presley on the wall of the establishment.

Ditka was generally very intense. Wannstedt was more laid-back and approachable. And Jauron was a serious tactician. All three wanted to win very badly. When he was on the field, Ditka was all football, but when he was off the field he knew how to have fun. —F.M.

Platteville Sights Seen

I will never forget: witnessing Steve McMichael deliberately running into and knocking over a Porta-Potty with an unsuspecting rookie inside during a practice break...Illinois State Police stopping Bears players for speeding home at the end of training camp, then asking the players for their autographs...William Perry sending his wife (at the time), Sherry, to the local Dairy Queen to pick up burgers and a bucket of french fries while he was supposed to be trying to lose weight on a special diet...Dennis McKinnon taking a swing at teammate Jim Harbaugh in the huddle during a practice scrimmage after a high pass left McKinnon exposed for a hard hit over the middle...Perry pancaking a rookie lineman on the first day of practice during the nutcracker drill...Ditka riding around in his golf cart watching practice while wearing a huge straw hat and smoking a cigar...Jim McMahon and Keith Van Horne tending bar downtown after curfew before bribing a security guard at the team dormitory to keep quiet. —F.M.

chapter 5

I Was an Offensive Lineman

Dan Jiggetts played for the Bears from 1976 through 1982.

Representing

I became a player representative at the end of my rookie year with the Bears. Our coach, Jack Pardee, suggested I become the rep after he learned I majored in government and economics at Harvard. I felt strongly that we had a solid players' association, but I didn't get paid a dime for that job.

Quite often being the player rep placed me in an awkward position. One time, for instance, one of our safeties, Gary Fencik, was fined for wearing his socks too high. It was brought up with the union, and eventually I think the league rescinded the fine on Gary. But Bears general manager Jim Finks became upset that our dirty laundry was being aired, so to speak. That was a small thing. The word around the league was that the guys who were spearheading these things didn't last very long.

Players today have no idea of what the journey was like to get them where they are now. In my playing days we tried to develop a partnership with the league. When we proposed receiving a portion of the proceeds, they called us communists. They said we were individual contractors. But it was quite an experience and I got to work with people like Gene Upshaw, Stan White, Ed Garvey, Tom Condon, and Mark Murphy.

You could see a labor fight brewing in the late 1970s. The issues on the table included free agency. The gross revenue was about giving us the pool of money, but defining player cost was a fuzzy number.

The owners thought there was no way we would strike during the season in 1982. We got the strike approval and we waited. Two weeks into the season, it was time to call the troops. About five weeks into the season, the owners realized we meant business. We reps went up to New York, and that is when it got really serious.

After we got the deal done and we circled around Halas Hall, I thought our guys would be practicing. But my teammates wanted to hear what the deal was before they went out to practice. The guys looked at the proposal. Then I got a call that the Lions, our next scheduled opponents, were not going to practice that day. That development led me to talking on the phone to the guys in New York. Meanwhile, Ditka was steaming. Eventually we went to Carmel High School in Mundelein, Illinois, and practiced under the lights.

All you had to do was win four games in that abbreviated season and you made the playoffs. After opening the season with a pair of losses before the strike, we beat the Lions 20–17. But we lost to the Vikings 35–7 before splitting the next four games.

It came down to the game at Tampa Bay. Ditka allowed us to have a New Year's Eve party in Tampa. It seemed to bring the team back together emotionally, but we ended up losing the game. Steve McMichael picked up a fumble late in the game and we thought he was going all the way, but Charlie Hannah brought him down and we lost 26–23.

The NFL had suffered its first work stoppage as seven games were canceled league-wide by the players' strike. The league decided to forego its traditional divisional rankings. Instead, the top eight teams in each division made the playoffs. The defending Super Bowl champion 49ers missed the playoffs with a 3–6 record, same as our mark. Detroit and Cleveland, a couple of 4–5 teams, made the postseason, but they were quickly eliminated. Dallas lost in the NFC Championship Game to Washington. The Redskins then beat Miami 27–17 in Super Bowl XVII.

That 1982 season was bizarre in a lot of ways. For instance, I remember it was suggested that players from both teams run to midfield and shake hands before the first two games following the end of the strike. It was supposed to be a show of solidarity with regard to the union. But that gesture was met by a round of boos throughout NFL stadiums.

Jim McMahon was named NFC Rookie of the Year in 1982, passing for 1,501 yards with a passer rating of 79.9. He became our starter as a rookie for the first game back after the strike. Due to the shortened season, Payton only rushed for 596 yards, but he averaged 4.0 yards per carry. He missed the Pro Bowl for the first time since 1975. Dan Hampton, another future Hall of Famer, recorded seven quarterback sacks in just nine games. Tight end Emery

Moorehead led our team in scoring with 30 points and in receiving yards with 363. Matt Suhey had the most catches with 36. Cornerback Terry Schmidt picked off a team-high four interceptions.

After seven years in the league, I came back in 1983 and the coaches switched my position from right tackle to guard when we were playing Buffalo. You really have to learn the nuances of the position to play it well.

I will never forget what Ditka said when he addressed our team before the first minicamp. He said: "The good news is, our goal is to win the division, conference, and Super Bowl. The bad news is, as I look out at you all, many of you won't be here to see it."

The second game of the preseason was in St. Louis. We went into overtime and I didn't see any action. I said my good-byes to the team; I knew I was gone. Our offensive line coach, Dick Stanfel, saw me and said, "How did you know?"

Believe me, I knew it was time. —D.J.

How Now Brown Cow?

Dan Peiffer was our center when I was playing with the Bears in the late '70s and early '80s. He was a tough son of a gun on the football field. But off the field, he was prone to, shall we say, *unusual* injuries.

Dan twice got his knee torn up when he was kicked by cows on his farm. Imagine that! I said to him, "Man, what are you doing to those cows?" He was a farmer down in Missouri during the off-season and he must have loved doing that. But he would come to camp every year and need another knee operation.

We had so much fun as a group of offensive linemen back in those days. With guys like Peiffer and Revie Sorey and Noah Jackson, we had a blast. Revie was so good-natured that it was easy to tease him and ride him about little things. I am so proud of what Revie has been able to do since his playing days, earning a master's degree in social work and doing so many great things in the community to help young people achieve in the classroom.

Revie has worked with the Ada S. McKinley Community Services Center, serving the community and sending minority students to major colleges around the country since 2000. Revie and that organization would go into tough high schools and set up plans to help those counselors identify the students who desperately want to go to college. Noah tended to be moody, but he could be hilarious at times. And I miss hanging around Peiffer and hearing about his barnyard tales from the farm. —D.J.

Age Is Just a Number

One of my favorite teammates with the Bears was linebacker Dan Rains. He recently revealed in a *Chicago Tribune* article that he lied about his age in order to enhance his chances of being signed as a free agent by the Bears.

A member of the Bears in the early 1980s and a backup to Hall of Fame linebacker Mike Singletary, Rains confessed that he fibbed about his age when he was signed as a free agent in 1982. I never knew that about Rains during our playing days. Rains explained his motivation for coming clean. He said that after watching the movie *Invincible* about a free agent player who made the roster of the Philadelphia Eagles, he felt like that movie was about him. Rains was 28½ years old when he signed with the Bears. He had told the Bears he was 23 at the time.

Rains, who now works for a contracting firm in Pittsburgh, played his college ball at the University of Cincinnati, redshirted his freshman year, then suffered numerous injuries. Once projected as a third-round pick, Rains fell off the NFL draft charts because of the injuries. So he went on to play semipro football with the Columbus (Ohio) Metros, the West Virginia Rockets, and other clubs. He even signed with a Canadian Football League team, only to fail the physical there. Just when he was about to try his luck with the United States Football League, Rains got a call from the late Bears general manager Jim Finks about a tryout.

Figuring he would have a better opportunity to make an impression as a 23-year-old recently out of college than a 28½-year-old, Raines lied about his age. But eventually his teammates discovered the truth.

Rains graduated from Hopewell High School with Tony Dorsett near Aliquippa, Pennsylvania. Rains was already in the NFL for a few years and Tyrone Keys was one of the Bears defensive linemen. They used to call Keys "Scoop" because he used to get newspapers from all over the country and read them. One day Keys called over to Rains's locker and said, "How old are you again?"

Rains said, "I'm 28."

Then Keys said, "How could you be 28 years old and Tony Dorsett is 34 when you played together in high school?"

That's who busted Rains; it was Tyrone.

Rains said he later shared his age secret with Singletary and asked him not to reveal it to the Bears coaches. Years later, Rains met up with former Bears defensive coordinator Buddy Ryan and came clean about his age. Buddy said, "How stupid do you think we are? We knew how old you were." —D.J.

Block Party

All of us linemen appreciated the opportunity to block for Walter Payton. We knew that if we could simply get in the way of a defender, Walter would be able to take care of the rest. We used to call them "get-in-the-way" blocks. If we could do that, Walter would make us look outstanding.

Whenever we ran a sweep, I figured we could get at least 10 or 15 yards. If Walter broke it, that would be gravy. We knew that Walter could handle the punishment of carrying 25 or 30 times a game. We did our best to just give him that opening to make something positive happen. When Walter broke all of those records and wound up as the NFL's all-time leading rusher at the time of his retirement, we felt like we were at least in part responsible. And that is also how Walter always made us feel. —D.J.

Remembering Papa Bear

One of my greatest pleasures in pro football was the opportunity to get to know George Halas. He was the real deal. It is amazing to realize how he was able to develop the Bears franchise from such humble beginnings. I remember walking around Halas Hall and hearing Mr. Halas call me into his office. He was always concerned about my career goals beyond football. He was interested in all of us as human beings, not just as football players.

Gale Sayers has especially fond memories of Halas. Of course, Sayers and Brian Piccolo were the first interracial roommates in the NFL. Piccolo died of a rare form of cancer in 1970 at the age of 26. The story of the friendship between Sayers and Piccolo was the basis for the award-winning movie *Brian's Song*.

For the first time in 36 years, the cast of that made-for-TV movie gathered in 2007 for a reunion and screening of the film to benefit the Gale Sayers Center. A lot of people don't realize that it was Halas who picked up the financial tab for Piccolo's medical bills, Sayers says. It turned out that the final hospital bill for Piccolo was over $500,000. And Halas took care of all of it. He also made sure that all three of Brian's daughters were able to go to college at Wake Forest, where Brian had been an All-American.

Paul Hornung, the Hall of Fame halfback and kicker for the Green Bay Packers, tells some great stories about his encounters with Halas. He said the greatest rivalry the Packers had was with the Bears. He loved to play against the Bears. Hornung would rather beat the Bears than anybody, as he did one season with a 52-yard free-kick field goal. Hornung also loved Halas, calling him "the greatest man in the history of the game." And Hornung knew that his coach, the legendary Vince Lombardi, loved and respected Halas as well.

The Bears and Packers would play each other three times a year back in the '60s—once during the exhibition season and twice during the regular season. Hornung said he ran the streets with former Bears Rick Casares, Ed O'Bradovich, and Mike Ditka during those many years. They played hard against each other on the field, and Hornung ran hard with them off the field. They had some great times. The Bears played their home games at Wrigley Field in the 1960s, and Hornung loved that venue.

Hornung takes credit for throwing the first football into the stands at Wrigley Field after he scored a touchdown. He said someone in the stands hollered for the football. For some reason, Hornung obliged. Halas called Hornung an unprintable name for his touchdown histrionics. Hornung said he loved that. And Lombardi yelled to Halas, "Don't worry about it. Hornung will pay for that football he threw up in the stands." —D.J.

Cutting It Close

One thing I noticed about the maturation of the Bears was the way the veterans took ownership and responsibility for the attitude and discipline of the team. That trend seemed to really take place in the middle and late '80s when the ballclub became very success-ful on a yearly basis. I recall a 1989 game apparently in hand for the Bears against the Cincinnati Bengals. But the Soldier Field crowd gasped with 1:29 left when young fullback Brad Muster fumbled the ball and the Bengals recovered with the Bears leading 17–14. Luckily for Brad, the Bears escaped with the win.

Dan Hampton, with tongue in cheek, said, "If I had a knife I would have stabbed him." Sure enough, Muster did improve when it came to holding onto the football. And Hampton realizes now that he is out of the game that patience is required when assess-ing young players. —D.J.

Great Scott

One of the most talented wide receivers on the Bears during my playing days with the ballclub was James Scott. He was fast, elusive, and possessed very good hands—all of the ingredients for a stand-out pass catcher. James also had that certain prerequisite swagger and confidence so many wide receivers seem to have. At times, it seemed, he had a bit too much swagger. James was into the whole image, from his immaculate Jheri curls to the way he dressed and the fancy cars he drove. Everything had to be just right. Appearance was everything to him. Perhaps a more disciplined Scott would have extended his NFL career.

When I saw James at Walter Payton's funeral in 1999, he had not changed much in appearance. Once he arrived with the Bears in 1976, Scott already had paid his dues to make it. Coming out of tiny Henderson State University in Texas, he was drafted in the eighth round by the New York Jets in 1975. But Scott wound up playing with the Chicago Fire of the old World Football League before getting an opportunity with the Bears.

It was beautiful to watch quarterback Vince Evans hook up with Scott on deep pass plays. We had so many fun-loving characters in those formative years of the Bears. I could tell at that time that the seeds of a Super Bowl championship team were being sown because of the attitude of young players such as Scott. —D.J.

In-Vince-Able

Vince Evans was a quarterback by trade. But early in his career, in order to get on the field, he was willing to return kicks to help the Bears. Vince had a fantastic throwing arm, but he also possessed great speed and a willingness to mix it up. At one point he was averaging about 20 yards per kickoff return, which was tops in the league at that time.

Nowadays, NFL teams wouldn't dream of having one of their young quarterbacks returning kicks. Vince got caught in the switches a couple of times, getting tackled pretty hard on the returns. I would be saying, "You can't be hitting our quarterback like that. He's our guy."

Vince had tremendous raw talent, and all he needed was somebody to help him harness that talent. But the Bears did not have someone working with him specifically to develop his skills,

Vince Evans was a quarterback ahead of his time.

one of the many reasons the team has struggled with the quarterback position over the years.

Vince could have been a great football player. He could have been a quarterback like Vince Young is today for the Tennessee Titans. Many of the Bears' passing records today are still held by Sid Luckman from the 1940s. What does that say about the Bears' dedication to improving that position?

Vince was the best man at my wedding and I was the best man at his wedding. We had a great deal of respect for each other. I was happy when the Raiders signed him to play after I recommended him. He really blossomed out there. —D.J.

Never Ever Surrender

One of the former coaches that I respected the most was Marv Levy, who coached the Chicago Blitz when I was there. The league was not rich in terms of great facilities and transportation modes, but it was rich in great experiences, thanks to people like Marv. From the south side of Chicago, Levy was one of seven inductees into the 2001 Pro Football Hall of Fame class and I was so happy for him. Levy joined former players Lynn Swann, Ron Yary, Jack Youngblood, Mike Munchak, Nick Buoniconti, and Jackie Slater in that class.

Levy was selected to coach the Buffalo Bills in 1986 after more than 30 years of coaching experience. He attended South Shore High School in Chicago before graduating from Coe College in Iowa, where he was a halfback on the football team and a member of the track team. His pro coaching odyssey began in 1969 as the kicking teams coach for the Philadelphia Eagles before he joined George Allen's staff as a special teams coach for the Los Angeles Rams in 1970. Then he moved on with Allen to Washington in 1971, where he served as the Redskins' special teams coach for two seasons. Levy then became head coach of the Montreal Alouettes of the Canadian Football League for five seasons.

I remember that Coach Levy had earned a master's degree in English history from Harvard, which is my alma mater. A poster of Levy's personal hero, Winston Churchill, would always hang in his office, with the quote, "Never, never, never surrender." —D.J.

A Legend Is Born

I was the Bears player representative and I spent a great deal of time working on the contract issues during the 1982 players' strike. Most of us player reps realized we put ourselves in a vulnerable position with league management, but we also felt that it was incumbent upon us to do the right thing for the betterment of the players. And today the players are reaping many of the financial benefits that we stuck our necks out to provide. When the strike was settled, I knew my days with the Bears as a backup lineman were numbered. I had been a right tackle all of my career and they asked me to move to guard that final year. I told them I would do whatever they asked me to do to remain on the team. But it didn't really work out.

George Halas, at the age of 86, apparently had one more major stroke of genius left in him when he hired Ditka as the 10th coach in the franchise's history in 1982 to succeed Neill Armstrong. Even though Ditka and Halas had butted heads in the past—forcing Halas to trade Ditka to Philadelphia in 1967—the love and respect between those two was undeniable. One year later, Jim Finks tendered his resignation and Halas appointed Jerry Vainisi as the team's general manager. Ditka, although he had no previous head coaching experience, was named NFL Coach of the Year in 1985, when the Bears went 15–1 in the regular season and coasted to three postseason triumphs, culminating in the 46–10 romp over the New England Patriots in Super Bowl XX.

Mike Ditka and George Halas are synonymous with Bears football.

The Bears won the NFC Central Division five consecutive seasons (1984–88) and reached the playoffs seven times during Ditka's tenure. From 1940 to 1943, Halas's Bears won four straight conference titles and three world championships. They outscored their opponents 1,313, to 540 during that span, recording a record of 37–5–1. In 1963, Halas coached the Bears to a world title, a 14–10 win over the New York Giants at Wrigley Field. But it was during the Ditka years from 1982 to 1992 that the Bears gained international acclaim. —D.J.

Manning Mauling

These days, Archie Manning is best known as the proud father of current NFL Super Bowl quarterbacks Peyton Manning of the Indianapolis Colts and Eli Manning of the New York Giants. But Archie was an outstanding quarterback in his own right. His biggest problem was that he played for the struggling New Orleans Saints most of his career. He finished with the Minnesota Vikings, and I recall the Bears really giving him a beating in 1984.

Archie called that game one of his most unpleasant memories in all of pro football. It was the worst beating he ever took. The Bears sacked him 11 times.

"For my money," Archie now says, "there has never been a defense tougher than the 1984 and '85 Bears. It was absolutely brutal. They were really something."

Early in his career with New Orleans, the Saints played us several times, but we weren't a whole lot better than the Saints in those days. As he looks back on his long career as a quarterback, Archie says playing in Chicago was always hard because of the weather, and the Bears always got after him real good. One time Archie had a good game against us when he ran for three touchdowns. Archie said he also thinks often about Walter Payton, whom he considered a great friend. —D.J.

chapter 6
The Sweetest Bear

Walter Payton set the standard for modern NFL running backs. His 16,726 rushing yards make him the league's second all-time leading rusher. (Photo courtesy of Bill Smith)

Meeting Walter

The first time I met Walter Payton was in 1976, the summer after I was drafted out of Harvard in the sixth round. I attended one of those Better Boys Foundation dinners in Chicago, and Walter was at the dais after receiving a Rookie of the Year award.

After the program, I went up to him to shake his hand. I said nervously, "I am looking forward to blocking for you." He gave me one of his patented firm handshakes and said, "Well, when are you going to start?"

That's how Walter was, and it was the beginning of a great relationship with him.

I learned early on that the best way to avoid being the victim of one of Walter's pranks was to stay close to him. In the locker room, Walter loved to roll up socks in a ball and fire them at people who weren't looking. And sometimes he would stick his head outside the door of the locker room and fire those rolled-up socks at somebody walking down the hallway at Halas Hall. One time, Jim Finks, the late Bears general manager, was walking down the hallway. He never saw the rolled-up socks that Walter fired at him. It was hilarious.

Walter loved cars, and I remember when he bought a midnight blue Lamborghini. A bunch of us linemen went over to his house to check out his new ride, but he wouldn't let us sit in the seats. He was afraid we would break the seats because we were so big. But Walter was always very generous to the linemen at the end of the season. He would always get us something nice. One year he got us pocket watches and another time he bought us some really expensive shotguns.

Walter and Roland Harper were inseparable. Harper was mainly used as his blocking back, but Roland was a hell of a player in his own right. In 1978, Roland rushed for 992 yards. He needed just eight yards to receive a bonus incentive. But he didn't get to touch the ball in the last game to have a chance at 1,000 yards. Years later I asked Roland how much that cost him. He said he would have gotten a $100,000 bonus. —D.J.

Walter Payton emerged from Jackson State University to become one of the NFL's most popular players. (Photo courtesy of Bill Smith)

Sweetness

Walter Payton was nicknamed "Sweetness" because of the beautiful way he ran with the football. And it certainly was a pleasure for me to block for him. But there also was a sweetness about him when it came to the way he dealt with people on and off the field. I remember one particular game in the early '80s against the Packers. Matt Suhey missed a block and Payton got clobbered head-on. He didn't have a chance to react. Walter was hunched over before he popped up off the ground and returned to the huddle as he always did. Instead of chastising his longtime friend and teammate in front of everyone in the huddle, Payton yelled over to the sideline: "I need a Darvon!" Then he glanced over at Suhey in the huddle and his smile turned to a more serious stare. He simply said to the Bears fullback, "Don't miss it again." The message was clear, yet Walter delivered it in such a classy way.

Walter loved Suhey, and Matt reciprocated that love by the way he stood by Walter's side until the very end of his life. I remember when the Walter Payton College Prep High School held its fifth annual "Drive to the Goal" fund-raiser on March 4, 2006. Mayor Richard M. Daley proclaimed March 4 (3-4, Walter's jersey number) "Sweetness Day" in the city of Chicago. The event was held at the Stadium Club at U.S. Cellular Field.

Walter's family was in attendance, including his mother, Alyne, his brother, Eddie, and his sister, Pam. Several of Walter's teammates attended, including Keith Van Horne and Richard Dent. Jim McMahon and Steve McMichael were honored by the Friends of Payton for their work with the students for Hurricane Katrina relief. McMahon and McMichael helped load truckloads of donations that were sent to Jackson, Mississippi, the home of the Payton family, where thousands of hurricane survivors are now living. Mike Adamle, another former Bears teammate, served as emcee and auctioneer for the event. —D.J.

Another Kansas Comet

Walter Payton became one of the greatest football players ever produced by tiny Jackson State University, but few people knew that he very well could have wound up at the University of Kansas.

Walter's older brother, Eddie, told me that Walter might have succeeded the great Gale Sayers as a Jayhawk had he not been sidetracked on his way for an official visit to Kansas. Walter decided instead to watch Eddie and his teammates practice at Jackson State, and he really loved the campus and the atmosphere there. That seemed to mean a lot to him. He could have played at any college in the country, but Jackson State was where his heart was.

The Bears drafted Payton in the first round, as the fourth overall pick in 1975. Payton rushed for 16,726 career yards, scored 110 touchdowns, and set a bunch of team records along

Walter Payton soars over the line of scrimmage against the New Orleans Saints. (Photo courtesy of Bill Smith)

the way. Additionally, his jersey number was retired, and he was inducted into the Pro Football Hall of Fame in 1993.

After he joined the Bears in 1975, it was frequently debated as to who was the better back—Sayers or Payton. It was generally conceded that Sayers was faster and more elusive, but Payton was incredibly durable and a more punishing runner. Both men wound up in the Hall of Fame with their signature styles.

Payton retired holding 26 Bears records and eight NFL marks. He was voted to the Pro Bowl nine times. The Bears led the league in rushing in 1977 behind the running of Payton, and then did not lead the league in that category again until 1983. The entire offensive line of Jay Hilgenberg at center, Tom Thayer and Mark Bortz at guards, and Jim Covert and Keith Van Horne at the tackles remained intact for seven years.

During Super Bowl XLI week, San Diego's LaDanian Tomlinson recalled watching Payton play on television. "I told my mother then that I wanted to be a football player," said Tomlinson, who was a co-recipient along with New Orleans quarterback Drew Brees of the Walter Payton Man of the Year award. —F.M.

Man Ready to Bite Dog

Walter Payton used to have a giant Schnauzer that he would sometimes bring around the team. One time, he had the dog in the locker room around the shower area. Bob Parsons, an end and punter on our team, was headed for the shower when the dog bit him hard, right in the rear end. Parsons, who had nailed an 81-yard punt that season, was extremely upset about this, as you might expect. At least he didn't try to kick the dog. —D.J.

Walter Payton excelled at keeping his teammates loose, both on and off the field.

Worth Watching

The thousands of people who adored Walter Payton as a football player also include current members of the NFL. Ahman Green, who starred for the Green Bay Packers before signing a lucrative free-agent contract with the Houston Texans in 2007, has always been a Payton fan. In fact, he told me he watches a tape of the "Pure Payton" video before every game he plays.

Green said, "That's something I have been doing since my third year in the league. In the regular season and the preseason, I haven't missed watching the video before a game."

I think it speaks volumes that Payton continues to have such a positive impact on fans and players, young and old. —F.M.

Shotgun Formation

In addition to playing football, Walter Payton had an affinity for fast cars and fancy guns. Walter bequeathed his extensive collection of guns to his son, Jarrett. Jarrett inherited the love of football and cars, but he decided the guns had to go.

"My dad was big into guns," Jarrett said. "I didn't know what to do with them. I am not a big hunter. I just feel that if you have something that someone else might cherish and have and main-tain and know what they are really about, then it is better to be able to give them to somebody else. For me, it's not something I am into."

Jarrett decided to put his father's guns up for auction in a facil-ity called Jennifer's Garden in Morris, Illinois. The collection included 54 guns, nine bows, a dozen fine hunting knives, and several Safari rifles. All of the knives have a serial number of 34, which was Payton's jersey number as a Hall of Fame running back with the Bears, and several of the guns have the serial number 000034. Proceeds from the auction became part of Jarrett's estate. —F.M.

Taking Mississippi by Storm

When he was 15 years old, Walter Payton huddled inside his parents' tiny house in Columbia, Mississippi, with his brother, Eddie, and his sister, Pam. Walter's parents, Edward and Alyne Payton, had opened their home to 48 desperate friends and relatives when Hurricane Camille swirled through the Gulf Coast town in 1969, uprooting trees and cars and hurtling dangerous debris. Eerie darkness engulfed them because electrical power was down for days.

"We had nowhere to go, nowhere to evacuate. It was frightening. Very scary," Eddie recalled. "And we didn't know how high the water was going to get around us. The worst feeling I have ever had. We were under about five feet of water and it pretty much drowned the entire town. It was one of those life experiences you never forget."

In the aftermath of Hurricane Katrina in 2005, Eddie referred to Jackson, Mississippi, as "the refugee center" for the people devastated by the hurricane in New Orleans and other parts of Louisiana and Mississippi. "We got about six hours of 65-mile-an-hour winds here in Jackson," he said as he helped neighbors clear overturned trees from their yards. "New Orleans got at least 110-mile-an-hour winds. And South Mississippi got about 90. There are more than a half million people in these parts without power. And we're one of them."

Eddie Payton talked about the possible damage Hurricane Katrina may have done to the high school football stadium in Columbia, Mississippi, named after Walter Payton. "We hope everything is fine after the hurricane. I don't know yet. But the football stadium, at this point, is the furthest thing from my mind," he said. "You can rebuild a football stadium. And if the Walter Payton statue is knocked over, we can put the statue back up. But human life is something you can't put a price on and you can't replace." —F.M.

The Ring, Please

Walter Payton used to refer to it as his "Ring of Truth," the audacious Super Bowl XX ring that commemorated the Bears' 46–10 victory over the New England Patriots in 1986. Several years ago, Walter volunteered to assist the Hoffman Estates High School basketball team in north suburban Chicago. He talked to them about the importance of trust and faith and not being afraid. To demonstrate the sincerity of his message, Payton removed the valuable ring from his finger and handed it to Hoffman Estates athlete Nick Abruzzo.

Payton told the young man to return it to him after a few days. But Abruzzo, who played both football and basketball at Hoffman Estates before moving on to play defensive end at Indiana University, did not return with the ring after fellow high school friends had admired it at his house. Payton was extremely disappointed, but remained gracious and continued to work with the youngsters in the program.

An eerily happy ending came about in 2001, however, almost two years to the day after Payton's somber memorial services. He died on November 1, 1999. "I have found Walter Payton's missing ring!" said Phil Hong, a Hoffman Estates alumnus, who was then a senior at Purdue University in West Lafayette, Indiana. "I was dumbfounded. It was so unreal to me."

Hong explained: "My dog was playing with one of its toys and it got stuck under the couch here. I went to get the toy out of there and the ring was sitting right there. It must have fallen out of the couch. These couches came from a buddy of mine, Joe Abruzzo. When I came to college, I took the couches that his family was going to throw out. Joe's brother, Nick, is two years older than us. When he was a senior at Hoffman Estates High School, his basketball team was going to the [Elite Eight tournament]. Walter Payton had given him his ring the day before to pass around for good luck. But they had lost it in their basement after school and it was never recovered.

"It started clicking in my head and I realized it was the couch that came from [the Abruzzos'] basement. The first thing I did was call up Nick Abruzzo. I said, 'Was that ring ever found in your house?' He said, 'No.' I said, 'Well, I've got it in my hand right now,'" said Hong.

"Nick told me that he was so glad that there finally has been closure put on that situation."

Hoffman Estates basketball coach Bill Wandro was pleased to know there was a happily-ever-after ending for this story, as well. "It's a great weight off my shoulders," Wandro said. "I knew the kids involved didn't do anything malicious. We supported those kids going on six years now. Just an amazing story. We tried to give everybody the benefit of the doubt. As a teacher and a coach, that is probably the biggest thrill about finding it. This is so amazing that the ring would show up like this. I think maybe Walter did us a big favor."

Two years after his passing, Payton continued to teach youngsters and adults lessons about faith and trust. —F.M.

Saying Good-Bye

Walter Payton always had a way of bringing out the best in all of his teammates—the best performances, the best laughs, and the best inspiration. It was that way during his Hall of Fame career, and that way again, sad to say, during his funeral. Virtually all of his former Bears teammates were there, alternately shedding tears and sharing hugs during a private memorial service at Life Changers International Church in Barrington Hills, Illinois.

I recall seeing many dignitaries, including Governor George Ryan and Mayor Richard M. Daley, among the mourners at the invitation-only private service. Former NFL commissioner Paul Tagliabue, who later told reporters that the NFL's Man of the Year award would bear Payton's name, joined relatives to pay final respects to the league's career rushing leader at the time. Club owners Ed and Virginia McCaskey and team president Ted Phillips headed up the Bears entourage.

Payton died of bile duct cancer, nine months after disclosing he had a rare liver disease. He was 45 years old. The public paid respects at the end of that week during a memorial service at Soldier Field, where Payton entertained so many during his 13-year career. His widow, Connie, and children, Jarrett and Brittney, were among family members who greeted friends during visitation prior to the services. A huge portrait of Walter in his Bears uniform stood behind them. Payton's body was cremated and his ashes sat in an urn on the altar.

Pastor Gregory Dickow told mourners, "This is a celebration of Walter Payton's life.... He is in a better place. He made his greatest gain on Monday when he died. He gained heaven. This is a celebration because this man, Walter Payton, is with his Lord Jesus Christ."

Payton's son, Jarrett, then a freshman football player at the University of Miami, eulogized his father in an emotional, anecdotal tribute. Jarrett recalled how difficult it was for his father to communicate with him in public because so many others tried to listen in on their conversations. From the time Jarrett was a young child, Payton would use a whistle in public to get his son's attention or to deliver a sign of encouragement.

When Jarrett played in his first college game against Boston College in 1999, Payton was too ill to attend the game. "But I swear I heard a whistle in the crowd, and I turned around and didn't see him. I will always remember that moment," said Jarrett.

"Many of you knew my father as a football player or business-man. I knew him as Dad. He was my hero. My mother, my sister, and I will miss him...but he is in a place where there is no sickness, no pain."

Eddie Payton, Walter's brother, thanked the media for its class in not going overboard in its disclosure of the terminal aspect of Payton's disease. Eddie then shared several humorous and sentimental stories about his famous brother. "My memory is a lot like my stature—short, but not bad," he said.

Walter Payton's son, Jarrett, and widow, Connie, look on during the memorial service held in Payton's honor at Soldier Field on November 6, 1999.

NFL sportscaster John Madden called Payton the "greatest football player I have ever seen. He was the total package. There are three kinds of people—those who make things happen, those who watch things happen, and those who don't know what's happening. Walter made something happen."

Mike Singletary emphasized Payton's courage and unselfishness "and acceptance of the Lord," in his remarks. Singletary also urged his former teammates not to wait for another such sad occasion to stay in contact. I certainly agree with that sentiment.

Mike Ditka quoted scripture as his voice cracked with emotion in describing Payton the football player and the person. "He was the best runner, blocker, teammate, and friend I have ever met," said Ditka. "I love Walter Payton. What is his legacy? It's the mark he leaves on all of us. That's better than scoring touchdowns. Walter was special. He was sweet."

I will always remember Walter as a gifted and hardworking athlete who had a lust for life that he shared with everyone he came to know. I truly miss him to this day. —D.J.

Carrying On Without Walter

During his happiest days, Payton was in perpetual motion. As a football player and as a businessman, he was constantly on the run, legs churning for that extra yard or that extra deal. Now his widow, Connie Payton, embraces Walter's lifestyle as she continues the charitable deeds he set in motion before his startling death.

"I probably could do something every day of the week if I wanted to," Connie tells me of her demanding slate. "My son, Jarrett, said, 'Mom, as much as you hate beepers, I think I am going to have to buy you a beeper to keep up with you because you are never home.'"

Nine years after her husband's death, Connie continues to adjust to his absence. "This may sound a little bit silly, but it still doesn't seem real," she said. "There are days when I just can't wait for him to pop up from behind a corner or a door, or something. I don't know if it is crazy on my part not to have fully accepted it, but it still doesn't seem real."

Connie constantly says that her husband did not die in vain, and I agree.

"I think the only satisfaction has been being able to do what we're doing—raising money for cancer research, continuing Walter's legacy with the foundation, and helping the kids with the Christmas fund and the after-school programs. There is a lot of comfort and inspiration to get up in the morning and keep going because there are so many great things to do," she said.

Connie Payton said she was unable to fully grasp the scope of Walter's celebrity before he passed away. "People will come up to me now and just start a conversation about Walter, be it man or woman. They think of Walter as if he was their best friend or family member. I don't know what happened to make them feel that way, but it is a great thing," she says. —F.M.

Sweet Memory

The memory of Walter Payton was recognized with the naming of McFetridge Drive near Soldier Field as Walter Payton Place in 2000. The honorary designation was voted by the Chicago City Council. Then it was time for the 2000 Bears players to truly honor the Hall of Fame running back by dedicating themselves to reviving the determination, courage, and relentlessness that were Payton's signature traits for 13 seasons in a Chicago uniform.

As a football player, businessman, and person, Payton never quit trying to reach for that extra yard, that extra edge to help the team or help another person less fortunate than himself. Walter once talked about how he felt less than physically superior as a young football player, but that hard work and a fear of failure drove him to the brink of his abilities. "You can't set limits for yourself. You have to constantly push yourself," he would say. "No matter what you do for a living, you know when you are doing your best or you are just mailing it in. When I am playing football, I want to leave it all out there on the field like it is the last game of my life."

A chance is all Payton ever wanted. —D.J.

chapter 7
Da Coach

Mike Ditka took over as head coach in 1982. His name would become synonymous with Chicago Bears football.
(Photo courtesy of Bill Smith)

Ditka Dynasty

Mike Ditka described his initial interview with George Halas for the head coaching position during an interview with Bob Sirott of WTTW, the public television station in Chicago.

"When I was coaching in Dallas, I wrote a letter to George Halas, telling him that at some point I wanted to be a head coach, and that I would love for him to consider me to be coach of the Bears," Ditka said. "Halas had me up for the interview at his kitchen table and asked me to tell him my philosophy on football. I said my philosophy was the same as him, to win. He said, okay, we're going to pay you X amount of dollars, and I said I'm sure happy to have the job. This was a lifelong dream to me."

I remember Ditka laying down new rules before our first mini-camp.

"We don't wear hats in meetings," Ditka told us. "I've got a couple of things I stand on, and one of them is wearing hats in meetings. Hats are for outdoors.

"You did everything we asked of you this weekend, and we asked a lot. Don't forget it, this is the way training camp will be. It's the way it has to be. I'll tell you this, this is a good football team standing here, and we're gonna get better.

"I played here when people really took pride in pulling on the Bears jersey. I want that to happen again."

I remember Gary Fencik's reaction to Ditka's initial message.

"That's something I never heard in the six years I've been here," he said. "We're always talking about being competitive. I'm glad someone's got a different frame of mind. I'm tired of being 'competitive.' Obviously, that attitude hasn't pushed us to our limits." —D.J.

Mad Dog

When Mike Ditka first took over as head coach of the Bears, he seemed to do everything by the stopwatch. Behind his back, we

Mike Ditka brought an old-school attitude when he took over the Bears in 1982.

gave him the nickname "Mad Dog." It wasn't a name you shared with him.

But unlike the other head coaches we had with the Bears, Ditka came in with a plan. He liked to run the football, which we liked as linemen. The only thing he tried to install that we didn't like was the "Dallas Shift." That was the maneuver the Cowboys used on offense when the linemen would stand up in unison, right before the snap count, to distract the defense with regard to the backfield formations. We could never get that shift right in practice with the Bears. We would look like an accordion, never standing up together at the right time. Ditka and his staff were thinking of trying to install the Dallas "Flex Defense" as well. But that never materialized.

I had been an offensive tackle throughout my college career and most of my NFL career. They switched me to guard when Ditka took over, and I had to learn a whole new position and new techniques. I got cut after the St. Louis preseason game. The game went into overtime and I didn't get off the bench, so I knew my time was up.

I had my exit interview. It was the first time I had been fired in my life. Little did I know it wouldn't be my last. I had to go home and explain that to my kids. Former teammates Vince Evans, Leslie Frazier, and Jim McMahon called me. I really appreciated hearing from those guys.

So I started to try to figure out what I was going to do. I didn't get one call from another NFL team. Nothing. So I went to play with the Blitz of the United States Football League. They asked me to help them in the front office, and they wanted me to play. Marv Levy, who would later become a Pro Football Hall of Famer, was the coach. Later on we had Bill Polian and John Butler come into the organization. Butler would always tell you straight. He was like your big brother.

Evans also later played with the Blitz. We signed four or five Bears who had been discarded, including Revie Sorey and Bob Parsons. —D.J.

Mike Ditka takes a break from the sideline atop a motorcycle.
(Photo courtesy of Bill Smith)

Tough Love

Former Bears quarterback Mike Tomczak once told me he was getting treatment from a sports psychologist to help him deal with the harsh criticism he received from Ditka. He said the sessions helped him maintain his personal confidence and perspective. Tomczak's mother, JoAnn, later said, "To me, it was the same as a businessman attending a seminar or something to help himself. That's the way Mike is; he's always trying to do something that will improve himself."

Ditka certainly wasn't the first coach to yell at Tomczak on the sideline. His father, Ron Tomczak, did his share of ranting when Mike played his high school ball at Thornton Fractional North in Calumet City, Illinois. "Mike thinks sometimes that Coach Ditka and I coach alike," Ron Tomczak told me. "Things were said, and that was it, and it was left right there on the field.

"I expected quite a lot out of him, and he did perform. He had pressure at that level, but it didn't affect him that much. The only thing he likes to know is that the person coaching him has confidence in him. He had a lot of pressure in high school and a lot of pressure at Ohio State."

In the last game before Ditka's heart attack in 1988, Tomczak screamed back at Ditka on the sideline during the 30–7 loss at New England.

Tomczak says he understands the occasional need to be chewed out, but "there's a time and a place for it," he said. "This was my fourth year in the league. Sometimes it motivates me and at times it just depresses the hell out of me. I know when I deserve it and when I don't deserve it."

You're a Double One!

For the most part, I got along well with Ditka, depending on his mood from day to day. Known for his short temper with the media, fans, and players alike, Ditka became increasingly impatient as the team failed to repeat as Super Bowl champions in the late 1980s. His reign with the Bears ended when the team went 5–11 in 1992.

One of the uglier exchanges between Ditka and the media involved the late Red Mottlow, who was a veteran radio sportscaster for WFYR-FM at the time. Ditka was holding his Monday morning press conference on December 10, 1990, in the basement of the old Halas Hall, and he was in an especially foul mood following a 10–9 loss at Washington that dropped the Bears' record to 10–3.

Here is the transcript of what ensued between Ditka and Mottlow. The press conference was cut short after six minutes.

Mottlow: "You just said, Mike, that with five turnovers and you don't score, there is something the matter."

Ditka: "Red...Timeout. We lost the game. So what? That's your problem, not my problem. You are the one who is offended by all of that."

Mottlow: "I couldn't care less, but what is the problem?"

Ditka: "What's wrong with the Miami Dolphins, who couldn't get out of their own way against them [the Redskins, in a 42–20 Washington win] the week before?"

Mottlow (interjecting): "I'm talking about the Bears and the Redskins."

Ditka: "Okay. They have got a pretty good defense. And they stopped us. Why don't you talk about how good they played instead of about our problems? Ahh, (bleep)! You're a joke."

Another TV reporter: "So, Coach, how will you adjust anything offensively against Detroit?"

Ditka (storming out of the press conference): "Nothing. We won't do a thing differently. And if you want to get answers to what you need, get them from Red Mottlow. He is an expert at everything."

Mottlow: "Thanks a lot."

Ditka: "I always try to appease a jerk."

Mottlow: "You're a double one." —F.M.

The Anti-Ditka

Longtime Bears media observer Brad Palmer refers to current Bears coach Lovie Smith as the "anti-Ditka" because of his laid-back demeanor. Compared to Ditka's well-known candor and emotion, Smith comes across as ultraconservative and at times secretive.

"It's like night and day. I mean, it's like banana split to vanilla ice cream. There is no topping or cherry or anything. We are just dealing with vanilla," said Palmer, who retired in January of 2006 following 40 years of broadcasting in Chicago. "Lovie doesn't even give it to you straight. I mean, Ditka gave it to you real straight.

"Ditka was renowned for his confrontational manner with the media. But with Ditka and me, it never got personal. I think we respected each other's point of view."

In Ditka's final year with the Bears, he again sparred with the media in an uncomfortable exchange. The line of questioning was

Mike Ditka won six NFC Central titles and a Super Bowl championship during his 11-year reign as head coach of the Bears.
(Photo courtesy of Bill Smith)

tentative at first, as writers and broadcasters sensed an agitated Ditka during his regular Monday press conference in Lake Forest on October 19, 1992. Even after an impressive 31–14 victory over Tampa Bay, Ditka appeared in no mood to provide in-depth commentary on the ramifications of the victory and the upcoming game at Green Bay. When radio sportscaster Tom Greene of WMAQ-AM asked Ditka whether he made a concerted effort to control himself on the sideline after Jim Harbaugh threw an interception, Ditka erupted in a profanity-laced tirade against the assembled media.

"No," Ditka responded calmly at first. "I didn't make a conscious effort to do that. I do it all the time."

Just two weeks prior, Ditka chastised Harbaugh along the sideline for calling an audible that led to a costly interception against the Minnesota Vikings. The following Sunday in the Tampa Bay game, Ditka walked away from Harbaugh when he came to the sideline following an interception by Darryl Pollard.

"I am going to say one thing to you people. We average how many plays a game? Would you guess 64 or 65? In six games, what does that come out to be? About 400. On 399 of the plays I have been calm. And on one I have been excited. Yet you sons of bitches made a big deal out of it. That's life," said Ditka.

"Remember that. One out of 400 I got excited this whole year. One! As long as you remember that, don't ever ask me another question about those things. Because I won't answer it and I will walk out of here. You want to talk about football, fine. If you don't, then you go somewhere else.

"Any one of you. All of you. You want to write about it, you go somewhere else. You want to talk about football, you talk about it. If you think this is a soap opera, you're [crazy]. Now, what else do you want to know?"

At that point, veteran sportswriter Phil Theobald of the (Peoria) *Journal Star* stood up and protested Ditka's obscene attack.

"Coach, I have respected you. I have never called anybody that name. And that is the first time I have ever been called that name," said Theobald, who then stormed out.

Ditka said, "I'm glad you respected me.... Anything else?" And then Ditka walked out.

The two passed each other in the basement corridor of Halas Hall and, according to Theobald, Ditka apologized, saying that he meant nothing personally toward him. —F.M.

Ditka's Health Scare

I was in Foxboro, Massachusetts, to cover a tough Bears loss against New England on October 30, 1988. Following that defeat, back in Chicago, Ditka suffered a more serious personal setback—a heart attack. Ditka returned to the sideline only 11 days later, although defensive coordinator Vince Tobin served as interim head coach for two games. Ditka now theorizes that his heart problem was attributed to stress more than anything. Doctors have said Ditka's heart attack was caused by a blockage of his right coronary artery. After Ditka was administered TPA (tissue plasminogen activator), a clot-dissolving drug, his artery opened up. Although there was a minimal accumulation of cholesterol and calcium deposits in the artery, it remained open.

There was some medical concern after Ditka's stress test that prompted the angiogram, which checked for blockage of arteries. "The procedure involved passing long, thin catheters through an artery that is present in the right groin area and normally goes down through the leg," said Dr. Jonathan Gilbert, who administered the test at Lutheran General Hospital. "Using an X-ray, we can advance that catheter up toward the heart and then selectively inject dye to the inside of the heart and see how the heart is contracting. We use a local anesthetic in the groin, and after that there shouldn't be any discomfort at all."

Ditka already was a workout zealot, lifting weights during vigorous early-morning routines. But then he began to talk about changes in his diet, and eating properly to cut down his fat and cholesterol intake was part of his new formula and routine. He also learned how to get more rest in addition to having some form of exercise. To this day, Ditka has maintained his healthier diet and lifestyle. He has tried drinking nonalcoholic beer, and he loves his red wine, which can benefit him health-wise.

Ditka jokes, "I always tell people I want to live to be 150 and they say, 'Why would you want to do that?' I say, 'Well, there's a few people I haven't made mad yet; I want to get them.'"

Ditka started a hospital-supervised cardiac rehabilitation program after his heart attack that included more sensible routines on the treadmill and stretching exercises. His wife, Diana, said she noticed some changes in her husband's demeanor as well. "He came home early two days in a row one week, and he went to bed very early," she recalled. "He came home and kissed me and the dog each time instead of kicking me and kissing the dog. He was very mellow."

Diana said that "Iron Mike" can be gruff and macho in public, but not necessarily so at home. "On the outside he is," she said. "Usually it's a two-minute temper, then he forgets what he gets mad about. He's going to be himself."

Ditka made a curious comment to reporters in his first interview after his heart attack. He said he felt "embarrassed" to have had a heart attack. "I think he was saying to himself, 'Did this really happen to me? I better take care of myself,'" said Diana. "It scared him, and it embarrassed him, too. He thought he was so healthy, and he thought he did all the right things. And then to have that happen to him...he couldn't believe it was happening. I think anybody's reaction would be that, 'Hey, this can't be happening to me. What have I done to deserve this?' I was thinking the same thing. I was really frightened. I couldn't believe this was happening."

Not too long after Ditka's heart attack, Bears players saw him stray from his promise "never to yell again." Cornerback Lemuel Stinson, then a rookie, ran into Minnesota Vikings punter Bucky Scribner in the regular-season finale. Ditka was in Stinson's face, yelling, stomping the ground, and grabbing his jersey as a national television audience witnessed "the new Mike Ditka."

Sorry, Coach. The players were trying their best not to rile you.

Mike Singletary remembers trying to get Ditka to settle down after the heart attack. But Singletary also knew that dealing with Ditka might make you his next victim.

Michael McCaskey, then the Bears president, cites Ditka's heart attack as the ultimate test of the organization's cohesiveness. "Everybody just pulled together," he said. "The players were determined to go out there and show that we could still win football games. Vince Tobin carried out his responsibilities as acting head coach in an admirable way."

As the mild-mannered team president, McCaskey was often overshadowed by Ditka's strong personality. When Ditka gently defied doctor's orders by returning to the sideline a little sooner than suggested, McCaskey had to consider the possibility of ordering him to continue resting.

"There's no question about it. The doctor said that it would be much better if he weren't on the sideline in Washington," said McCaskey. "But Mike wanted to do it. There is an area of thought in medicine that a patient is best served if he or she takes a fuller measure of responsibility for the course of treatment. Mike clearly did that."

In humid central Florida, where man is often pitted against the elements, Ditka and the Bears survived the oppressive heat and the bothersome Tampa Bay Buccaneers to win 27–15. In his first game back as head coach after recuperating from the heart attack, the new and improved Ditka unveiled himself to 67,070 fans and an admiring audience of television viewers that included his cardiologist, Dr. Jay Alexander. Following doctor's orders, Ditka generally tempered his emotion and bottled his reaction to such previously intolerable indiscretions as dropped passes by Bears receivers, interceptions thrown by Bears quarterbacks, and six fumbles by his good-hands people. —F.M.

Playing Without Heart

A healthier Ditka and his Bears entered 1989 hoping to build on the previous year's success, but challenges and difficulties lay ahead. Ominous signs appeared during the preseason. Following a 22–17 exhibition loss to the Kansas City Chiefs, Ditka let his players have it. From both an aesthetic and athletic standpoint, Ditka was not pleased with the loss. I remember hearing Ditka rant: "We stunk; we absolutely stunk. We couldn't do the basic things you have to do to protect the quarterback. Countless penalties...can't make a field goal from 27 yards...turnovers, fumbles, dropped passes. We stunk up the football field."

Ditka was in midseason form after the Bears' second straight sloppy performance. I remember him steaming: "Something is going to happen. Either we're going to get our butts whipped real bad this whole year or somebody better wake up, because we're not nearly as good as we think we are. There are a lot of guys in there who think they are.

Later, Ditka said, "We will either do it my way or we won't do it. No more their way. I'm tired of hearing how good people are. I want to see them play from now on. I don't care if they are backups, understudies, undergraduates, or what they are. A lot of those guys are not going to be with us after tomorrow. I had a lot of remorse in my heart going into this about cutting people. I don't have any after watching some of them play. They were terrible. We've done this for two weeks in a row. We lined up with backup people, and we can't play a lick. We put a quarterback in there, and his life is in his own hands. We go forward for a first down, and then we go backward.

"You might get the gist that I'm aggravated. And I'm going to stay aggravated until January."

So much for a more mellow Ditka taking it easy after his heart attack. —D.J.

Sympathy for Native Son

I visited Ditka's hometown of Aliquippa, Pennsylvania, following his firing by the Bears in January 1993. That provided me a unique perspective of this complex man. Barely a week after Bears president Michael McCaskey pulled the plug, Ditka's dismissal started to hit home in Aliquippa. Frank Marocco, a high school teammate of Ditka's who became the football coach at Aliquippa High School, said Ditka's firing reminded him of when President John F. Kennedy was assassinated, at least from the perspective of the folks in Aliquippa. He said a hush went over his hometown, the same way a hush went over the country when Kennedy was shot in 1963.

Marocco also said that when a hometown guy like Ditka is emotionally wounded by being fired, his entire hometown community feels the pain. From the mostly blue-collar patrons of Papa Duke's Paris Grill to the truck drivers and greasy-uniformed mechanics in Harry's Cafe, the lifelong residents of the town of 17,094 remained solidly entrenched in Ditka's corner.

Marocco went on to say he realizes pro football is a vicious business that is fueled by the same kind of politics that govern any major corporation. He said that if people want you out badly enough, they'll get you out.

Ditka's roots run deep in his hometown. His parents, Mike Sr. and Charlotte, are now deceased. In 1993, they continued to reside in a tiny, humble abode atop Linmar Hill, overlooking the city. I remember Mrs. Ditka telling me that they had lived in that same house for 51 years. They had planned to buy a new house at one point, but Mike wanted to stay in the same neighborhood so he could attend Aliquippa High School. The living room was neat and small, cluttered with high school pictures of Mike in his 1950s crew cut. Photos of his brothers and sisters also were positioned on the television set, with no special preference to Mike.

Mike Sr., an ex-marine who became a railroad worker, said he never dreamed his son would perform as well as he did with the Bears during his 11-year coaching stint. Charlotte Ditka counseled her son after his firing by telling him everything happens for a reason, even though she could tell by his tears that he was truly hurting. Like most parents, Mike and Charlotte Ditka simply wanted their son to be happy, whether he decided to rest for a year, return immediately to coaching, or pursue another goal. Ditka was 53 at the time, so it was difficult for Mike Sr. to tell his son what to do, Mr. Ditka said to me. But he wanted his son to take a year off, get one of his hips replaced, and play some golf.

The stories have become legendary for Ditka's lifelong friends in Aliquippa. When he was seven years old, Ditka smoked his first cigarette behind his parents' government-subsidized house. He accidentally set the backwoods on fire. Paul Dinello, who later became superintendent of schools in Aliquippa, remembered that he and Mike were both altar boys down at a Catholic church. He described Ditka as "a very high-intensity boy." Dinello and Ditka played Little League together. He said Ditka could not accept defeat whatsoever, even at a young age. He was committed to winning. Even as a boy, he threw tantrums or would cry uncontrollably. The only one who could control Mike, according to Dinello, was Mike's mother.

Charlotte Ditka remembered her son's passion for sports as a youngster. She told me she remembered when Mike played with a brace on his back and shoulder for a whole year. His father noted that Mike was very emotional as a kid, especially after a loss or a mistake. Ditka's mother said her son always watched the movie *It's a Wonderful Life* with Jimmy Stewart and Donna Reed on Christmas Eve. She said Ditka would come out into the kitchen and his eyes would be all red and puffy.

Also, Ditka could not tolerate other people making mistakes, Dinello said. He recounted the story of Ditka chasing his brother, Ashton, home after he dropped a routine fly ball in the outfield that cost their team an American Legion baseball game.

Dinello said the Bears got rid of the "mouthpiece of the NFL" when they fired Ditka, although Ditka has managed to parlay his coaching success and popularity into lucrative media gigs and endorsement deals. Ditka has shared his good fortune with his old community: he has conducted an annual golf tournament in Aliquippa that raises $15,000 to $20,000 for local charities and establishes scholarships for high school students, and he contributed $100,000 to the University of Pittsburgh, where he was an All-American as a tight end, linebacker, and punter. The same area that spawned future NFL stars Joe Namath, Jim Kelly, Joe Montana, and Dan Marino is proud of Ditka and his legacy. —F.M.

In Life...

During his final years as head coach of the Bears, Mike Ditka became increasingly philosophical and he had a tendency to lecture to the assembled media during press conferences. His favorite opening phrase was: "In life..."

The predictability of Ditka's opening line encouraged me one day to enlist my fellow scribes in a wager as to the exact point and time in his postpractice monologue that the "In life..." phrase would pop out of his mouth. Each writer at Halas Hall plopped down a dollar bill while picking a time—30 seconds, 45 seconds, a minute, or whatever—when they thought the phrase would be used.

At just under a minute into his postpractice spiel, Ditka came through for me and I collected $10. When the writers erupted as he uttered the famous words, Ditka looked around the pressroom puzzled, but not quite aware that he was the unwitting cause for the commotion. Of course, Da Coach had many famous quotes over the years, including the one about the past being for "cowards and losers."

Here are a few other famous last words from Ditka:

—"If things came easy, then everybody would be great at what they did, let's face it."

—"Success isn't measured by money or power or social rank. Success is measured by your discipline and inner peace."

—"Success isn't permanent and failure isn't fatal."

—"You're never a loser until you quit trying." —F.M.

chapter 8
The '85 Bears

The 1985 Bears immortalized themselves in the "Super Bowl Shuffle."

Shy of Perfection

I held my breath as the New England Patriots were perched on the doorstep of NFL history, just a Super Bowl victory shy of becoming the first team to finish with a 19–0 record after ending the regular season undefeated at 16–0. But the New York Giants upset the Patriots in Super Bowl XLII to end that dream.

The Bears had two undefeated teams in their franchise history before the 16-game regular season was introduced. In 1934, the New York Giants upset the 13–0 Bears, 30–13, in the NFL Championship Game. In 1942, the Bears posted a perfect 11–0 record and outscored their opponents 376–84. The Bears were favorites to win their third consecutive title when they met the Washington Redskins in the 1942 NFL Championship Game. However, the Redskins upset the Bears 14–6. Two years before, the Bears had humiliated the Redskins 73–0 in the title game.

The 1985 Bears were 12–0 before the Dolphins knocked them off 38–24 on *Monday Night Football*. Those Bears finished 15–1 in the regular season and coasted to a Super Bowl XX title, crushing their three postseason opponents by a combined score of 91–10.

The '85 Bears were recently ranked the second greatest Super Bowl championship team on the NFL Network's documentary series *America's Game: The Super Bowl Champions*, behind only the '72 Dolphins. ESPN rated the '85 Bears as the greatest NFL team of all-time.

The 1972 Miami Dolphins publicly celebrate when other teams fall short of their perfect regular-season mark, which was 14–0 in that era.

Supporters of the '85 Bears point out that the '72 Dolphins played an easier schedule. No opponents on the '72 Dolphins schedule made the playoffs, and nine of their 14 foes finished with a sub-.500 record. Miami finished 17–0 culminating with a 14–7 Super Bowl victory against the Redskins.

Mike Ditka's '85 Bears, on the other hand, allowed the fewest points (198) in the NFL that year as they did not permit their opponents to score more than 10 points in 11 of their 16 regular-season games. Offensively, those Bears scored 456 points, which was second in the league.

This was a brash, presumptive collection of characters who dared tape the "Super Bowl Shuffle" video midway through the regular season. Would Chicagoans be more tolerant today if their '85 Shufflin' Crew joined the '72 Dolphins in celebration when another team approached regular-season perfection? There is no doubt in my mind Chicagoans would not only embrace that notion, but most would join in the party. —D.J.

The Battle of New Orleans

Mike Ditka relaxed the rules for his players during Super Bowl week in New Orleans in January 1986. Former Bears kicker Kevin Butler, who was a rookie that season, remembers what it was like the week before he kicked three field goals as the Bears demolished New England 46–10 in Super Bowl XX. He said, "When we got there in New Orleans, it seemed like the town was full of Chicago people. The excitement was just as high on Monday—a week before the Super Bowl—as it was on Sunday.

"The main rule was just don't get caught and put in jail," Butler recalled. "That was the main thing for that team. There were some nights when we didn't have any curfew. Coach Ditka didn't change his rules from how he conducted his team all year long. He left a lot on that team to govern itself.

"It was a team that would play hard, would party hard, would be out late. But the closer it got to the game, it just tapered back and everybody got into that state of mind that separated us from everybody."

Jim McMahon was at the center of most of the Super Bowl week controversy. Butler recalls that he spent a lot of time with McMahon that week. Butler confirmed that McMahon certainly dropped his pants and mooned a helicopter that was hovering above their practice. Butler was warming up next to McMahon, so he had a nice view of that, too. McMahon also had acupuncture procedure done while in New Orleans. —F.M.

Oops!

Ditka often has said he regrets not calling a play to give Walter Payton an opportunity to score a touchdown in Super Bowl XX when the Bears were in close scoring position. Walter, being the class act that he was, never seemed to hold any resentment about that missed opportunity.

"It would have been great to score one," Payton told me years after Super Bowl XX. "In the days and weeks after the game, yes, I was bothered by it. But I was blessed to have parents who instilled in me that things happen for a reason. You may not understand it when it first happens, and it might not be something that you're going to be happy about, but down the line there will come a time when it will be shown to you."

One of the only mistakes the Bears made in Super Bowl XX was not getting Walter Payton into the end zone.

Quarterback Jim McMahon scored on a one-yard touchdown plunge in the third quarter of Super Bowl XX. "On the touchdown that I scored, it was a play designed for Walter, but the truth is I don't think anyone recognized it during the game. I know I didn't," McMahon now says.

Ditka said he was too caught up in the euphoria of the game to immediately notice that Payton had not scored a TD. "I really didn't realize it. I never thought about the individual thing so much," Ditka said. "That was stupid on my part. That was probably the most disturbing thing in my career. That killed me. If I had one thing to do over again, I would make sure Payton took the ball into the end zone. I loved him; I had great respect for him. The only thing that really ever hurt me was when he didn't score in the Super Bowl."

Connie Payton said she has sympathy for Ditka, who has to answer questions about why Walter did not get a chance to score a touchdown from close range in Super Bowl XX. "I think it bothered Walter a little bit. But he got over it," she says now. "My thing is, 'You won it!' So it shouldn't matter. It would have meant a lot, but it didn't take a lot to get over it. I feel so bad for Coach Ditka. Everyone brings that question up to him and he has apologized so many times. Really, you get caught up in the moment. They were all caught up in the moment. But he won it and got a great ring to prove it." —F.M.

The Team of the '80s

The projected Bears dynasty lasted all of one glorious season, leaving the San Francisco 49ers to claim the title as the NFL Team of the '80s. Joe Montana, who quarterbacked the 49ers to four Super Bowl triumphs, remembers the '80s as the best time of his life.

"I think there were a lot of great teams during that time. One of them was coached by Bill Parcells, then of the Giants," Montana said. "I think the [reason] there was so much fun in the '80s is that there was so much competition around. There were times when you could take a look at whether it was going to be us or the Los Angeles Rams in our division. Or the Redskins or the Giants or the Cowboys in the NFC East. I think when [the NFL] tried to get a little more parity, in some cases they lost a little bit of the excitement."

The 1985 Bears finished the regular season 15–1 before trouncing the New England Patriots 46–10 in Super Bowl XX. But the Bears subsequently lost key free agents such as Wilber Marshall and Willie Gault, and quarterback Jim McMahon was constantly battling injuries.

"There are not so many good teams around now, and I don't know why that has happened," said Montana. "I think back then...that was the best time to be in the NFL. I think we had the best of all worlds in playing some great football teams and not just some very good ones. When you look at the Bears and the Giants, they were as good as they come. And you can never take out the Cowboys and Redskins. It was just a fun time. I don't know why we ended up dominating, but I was glad we did. Or we perceived that we did." —F.M.

Super Bowl Denied

As rewarding as my experience with the Bears turned out to be, I certainly would have liked to have been a part of the 1985 Super Bowl Bears. It just wasn't to be. However, a different set of circumstances conspired to prevent Al Harris and Todd Bell from being a part of that Super Bowl team. Both Harris, represented by agent Ethan Locke, and Bell sat out the entire 1985 season and Super Bowl XX because of contract disputes.

Sadly, safety Todd Bell passed away March 16, 2005, at the age of 46. Harris still lives in Chicago, and I spoke to him recently.

After missing one full season, Harris returned to the Bears in 1986, but he told me it took him until 1988 to get over the holdout because he felt disconnected from the rest of the organization. There was a period of time when he felt sorry for himself.

Harris says he is at peace now with the controversial business stance that unfortunately has marred his otherwise stellar playing career with the Bears. He bravely decided to remain in Chicago after his playing days to face the constant questions about his decision. He says he feels blessed to have a wonderful family and friends and to have had an outstanding NFL career. So he does not mourn his career.

"It would have been very easy for me to leave the city of Chicago because this gets brought up to me all the time," he said. "The Super Bowl is a great achievement, but it is not going to make somebody happy. That's the way I look at it....

"Yes, I missed the Super Bowl. But I played 11 years in the best league in the world. And I was able to come back [after the holdout] and play five more years. So I had five more years to win the Super Bowl [with the Bears and Eagles]. I am happy with my career and I am happy with who I am. Some people don't want me to be happy, but that's their problem. That's who I am and I am at peace about it."

In his 11 seasons in the league, Harris played with the Bears and the Eagles, and he has a healthy perspective on life. He was taken aback in 2007 when he saw that linebacker Lance Briggs initially turned down a contract offer from the Bears for $7.2 million after he made $700,000 the year before. "I would have done cart-wheels and backflips if the Bears had offered me 10 times what I had made in 1984," said Harris, who also played defensive end during his career.

Harris performed well for the Bears in 1984, but the team had drafted Wilber Marshall out of Florida in the spring of '84, paying him nearly $500,000 a year. "Our '84 defense was number one in the league and we went to the NFC Championship Game in San Francisco," said Harris, a first-round pick out of Arizona State in '79. "I was 27 at the time and still a young player. Then they gave Wilber almost $500,000 a year, which was a ton of money back then. So here we had Wilber sitting on the bench, and I am starting in front of him. So then my contract is up and he is making three times as much as me. So we start to negotiate and I want something close to what my backup has. They offered me only half of that. Things were said and things were getting kind of emotional behind the scenes and I took it personal. When you make it personal, that makes negotiations doubly hard. When a guy feels disrespected, now you have a double whammy to deal with."

In retrospect, Harris now realizes the Bears "were in a funny position" with the desire to get Marshall on the field in 1985. "First of all, my situation wouldn't have even happened today because I would have been a free agent and I could have gone to another team. That was just part of the agreement that needed to be changed. Was it fair in my eyes? No, but that's how it worked out and it opened the door for Wilber, and the rest is history." —D.J.

Leslie's Luck

Talk about bad timing.

Leslie Frazier's NFL career ended prematurely when he tore up his knee returning a kick for the Bears after they had a commanding lead in Super Bowl XX. The final score was 46–10.

Now the defensive coordinator of the Minnesota Vikings, Frazier might have better timing when it comes to filling a head coaching vacancy. His name has figured prominently in a few head coaching discussions as of late. "It's so weird, you know. To first of all get back to this game as a coach, as opposed to being a player," Frazier says now. Frazier led the Bears in interceptions in each of his last three seasons, finishing his career with 20 in 65 games. Previously serving as an assistant with the Super Bowl champion Indianapolis Colts and as defensive coordinator for the Cincinnati Bengals, Frazier began his coaching career at Trinity College in Deerfield, Illinois. He also served as secondary coach at the University of Illinois before joining the Philadelphia Eagles in the same role. A quiet, spiritual man in the mode of Indianapolis Colts head coach Tony Dungy, Frazier found himself being more than an assistant coach in 2005 when Dungy lost a son to suicide.

Leslie Frazier is helped off the field after injuring his knee during Super Bowl XX.

"When Tony first talked to me about joining his staff, one of the positives that I thought about was the relationship that I had with him prior to him asking me to coach with him," said Frazier. "I thought I could bring our friendship to the table and help him with his football staff.

"When the tragedy of his son's death occurred, that was a very, very difficult time. And I saw where my being there was so important from a personal standpoint, more than a football standpoint. Just to be there to support him, like so many have done. Just watching how he handles adversity, and then how he has handled success…. It helps you a great deal."

An eventual return to the Bears organization for Frazier in some coaching capacity would not be out of the question. "Man, I would love that," said Frazier. "I remember before I left Trinity and I was trying to make the decision whether to come back [to Trinity] and make that my career, or take that leap of faith to go to the next step. I went to lunch with [Bears chairman] Mike McCaskey one day and we were just talking about making that decision.

"I said, 'I hope that one day if I decide to leave Trinity, I can come back and work with the Bears and help the team achieve great success.'

"He said, 'Well, I would love nothing more than for that to happen.'

"Now 10 years later, I am in a different situation.... Maybe one day, who knows? It would be great to get back to Chicago." —D.J.

Once Was Not Enough

While Mike Ditka's Super Bowl team stands out as one of the finest in franchise history, the fact that the core group of players was unable to repeat as champions continues to frustrate those players and Bears fans. I was not fortunate enough to be a member of the Super Bowl XX team, having been released two years earlier. However, I have had an opportunity to talk to a lot of my former teammates who did make it.

Former Bears wide receiver Willie Gault laments that the 1985 Bears were the youngest team ever to win the Super Bowl at that point, averaging about 24 years of age. Gault felt that nucleus should have won two or three more titles. But he feels blessed to have been a key member of one Super Bowl squad, noting that many great players such as Dan Marino never earned a Super Bowl ring.

While the New England Patriots have enjoyed their run of Super Bowl titles, former Bears safety Dave Duerson thought about the Bears' one-and-done title chase. Duerson also earned a Super Bowl ring with the Giants. Duerson told me how much he respects New England Patriots head coach Bill Belichick, who was an assistant coach with the Giants under Bill Parcells in 1990. Belichick was the defensive coordinator and secondary coach when Duerson picked up his second Super Bowl ring.

Duerson feels strongly that the reason Belichick has enjoyed so much success with the Patriots is that he comes from the Parcells system, which is a system that demands excellence. They have hard, aggressive practices. They don't care if you are the marquee player or the low man on the totem pole—you have to work every day. You are not taking days off. You certainly are not going to be put on injured reserve for a bad finger or something small like that. Belichick is a guy who demands the maximum out of his players.

As time passes, Duerson said he gains a greater appreciation for his Super Bowl wins. He calls those championships the ultimate in pro sports, and certainly within the National Football League. It happened, he said, because a group of guys came together and parked their egos long enough to achieve a common goal. The Bears were able to do that in '85. It was a team blessed with all sorts of incredible talent, but unless the coach and team can pull that talent together and have everybody focused in the same direction, your ability to achieve is diminished. Without chemistry, the Bears would have been just another great defensive team that didn't get it done. But they were able to reach the ultimate goal in '85. The same thing happened when Duerson was in New York with the Giants. They were a bunch of old guys who had all lost a step. But they were able to get it done because they stayed together and focused on one goal, which was, first of all, to dominate and control their division, and then take each playoff game one at a time. When they got to the Super Bowl against the Buffalo Bills, they were poised to win it all. —D.J.

Trying to Make a Dent

Richard Dent says he was "not the chosen one" when it came to being publicly praised and promoted by the Bears organization, and that has adversely affected his bid to be selected for the Pro Football Hall of Fame. The Bears' all-time leader in quarterback sacks and the Super Bowl XX MVP has been among the finalists for the Hall of Fame the past several seasons and is hoping to eventually crack the barrier.

Richard Dent was the MVP of Super Bowl XX.

An eighth-round draft pick out of Tennessee State, Dent was a four-time Pro Bowl selection who also played for the 49ers, Colts, and Eagles. He wound up his 15-year career with 137.5 sacks, eight interceptions, 13 fumble recoveries, and two touchdowns.

"There were many years when me and Mike Ditka used to go at it. I used to tell him, 'If you don't like me, get rid of me. If you think you can find something better, you can give the job to them.' I used to tell him that all the time," said Dent.

Dent said Ditka is now in his corner as a Hall of Fame candidate, but he fears the damage already has been done in terms of trying to promote his credentials to the Hall of Fame committee. "Mike feels I should be in the Hall of Fame," said Dent. "When I saw him at the Super Bowl this past year, he said, 'Richard, I am sorry you didn't make it in. But we are going to get you there.' But sometimes what happened in the past screws up the present times."

In 1985, Dent recorded 17 sacks, intercepted two passes, and recovered two fumbles. Former teammates Walter Payton, Mike Singletary, and Dan Hampton already have been enshrined in the Pro Football Hall of Fame. "Dan was a good player, but I think the times we were playing in the league, people on the other teams always said that the two [Bears players] they wanted to knock out of the game were me and Walter. They wanted to stop Walter and they wanted to stop me. It is nice that your peers look at you that way," said Dent.

"I think I was a major part of the Bears for many years. I was not the chosen one for the Bears to promote. Nothing against the guys that I played with; it's not their fault. The organization was putting their money behind certain guys. I was a guy who came in [203rd overall pick] and you already had [first-round picks] Hampton and Al Harris where you had paid money and drafted people. If you come in and take out one of those [high] draft picks, then what you are doing is you are kind of causing problems."

In the 1984 and 1985 seasons, Dent recorded a total of 34½ sacks. —F.M.

Punky QB

One of the most popular Bears players of the 1980s was Jim McMahon, known as the "Punky QB." McMahon played with many injuries during his career and helped the '85 Bears win the Super Bowl. But when he was unable to play, the team suffered dearly and perhaps that is why that core group did not win more than one title.

McMahon remains a bit of a folk hero to Bears fans, even though McMahon admits he pays little attention to the NFL these days. These days he spends most of his time with his family and golfing—barefoot, of course—all over the country.

I will never forget the catchy lyrics to the "Super Bowl Shuffle" that was produced by Red Label Records:

I'm the punky QB, known as McMahon.
When I hit the turf, I've got no plan.
I just throw my body all over the field.
I can't dance, but I can throw the pill.
I motivate the cats, I like to tease,
I play so cool, I aim to please.
That's why you all got here on the double,
To catch me doin' the Super Bowl Shuffle.

In the 1980s, Michael Jordan and Jim McMahon dominated the Chicago sports scene.

I remember when I got cut from the Bears in '83 and McMahon was one of the few former teammates to give me a call soon afterward. He said he was sorry to see me go. Then, before he hung up, he asked me: "What was the name of that guy who can get us a pool table?" —D.J.

Should Have Signed the Dog!

Steve McMichael was one of the all-time fascinating characters in the storied history of the Bears franchise. "Mongo," as everyone called him, remains proud of his stamina during his 13-year career as a defensive tackle. He never missed a game—191 in a row. He says he has a great appreciation for his durability, and people should have a greater appreciation of him because of how long he played the game.

"It's a yearlong job. You work out hard. You don't get all those little injuries," he said. "I think this is where these new kids are missing the boat. You want to relax and take it easy, but after you get out of the game and you look back on it, you say to yourself, 'Man, that happened so fast. Why didn't I do more?' You're going to look in the mirror one of these days and you aren't going to like the person you see in it."

McMichael recalled his long road to glory with the Bears. It took some time for him to impress Bears defensive coordinator Buddy Ryan. "New England had cut me and it was six weeks into the season when the Bears called me up to replace an injured defensive lineman," he said. "Well, [veteran] Alan Page never practiced. So I realized that first day that I was going to have every play of that practice. Before the practice started, Buddy Ryan came up to me and said, 'Hey, No. 76, we're going to work your butt off today. Have you been staying in shape?' I said, 'Yeah, I've got this big black Great Dane. And me and him have been jogging.' After practice I am bent over and gassed after wind sprints. And I could hear Ryan coming up from behind me saying, 'Shoot, No. 76, we should have signed the dog.'" —F.M.

Steve McMichael was one of the true Monsters of the Midway during his Bears career.

Covert Activity

I was fortunate to block for Walter Payton in the late '70s and early '80s, along with a dedicated crew of offensive linemen. But former Bears tackle Jim Covert came along in 1983 and would be named to the NFL's All-Decade team of the '80s because of his well-respected blocking techniques, strength, and skill.

I was proud of the fact that the Bears led the league in rushing in 1977 behind the running of Payton. The Bears did not lead the league in that category again until Covert's rookie year of '83. The entire offensive line of Jay Hilgenberg at center, Tom Thayer and Mark Bortz at guards, and Covert and Keith Van Horne at the tackles remained intact for seven years.

"Yeah, that was pretty amazing," Covert recalled. "We led the league in rushing four straight years. Fans today have to be true pro football fans to keep up with all this player movement throughout the league. I played my entire career with one team and I had several teammates who did. So now is a difficult era to coach in, as well."

Since the time I played for the Bears, there have been major differences in offensive line techniques employed. Covert says he sees big differences as well. "I see that they have the biggest possible human beings they can get, and they put them on the offensive line," says Covert. "Then they go straight ahead. They zone block. Very rarely do you see guards pull out in space. I was a tackle and we would run those 'counter-OT' plays and I would pull seven, eight, nine times a game. Jay Hilgenberg, our center, would pull on a lot of plays. Our guards would pull a lot with the sweeps we used to run. You don't see that anymore. You just see the big guys going straight ahead. The other thing that bothers me a little bit is the way they pass protect. Nobody gets their hands up; nobody gets their head back to block. Nobody punches anymore. They are so big that they just sort of absorb everything."

If Covert were still playing today, he would have to line up at guard instead of tackle. "My rookie year I came in at 290 pounds and Coach Ditka wanted me down to 275. He said he thought that was the weight that I played my best football." —D.J.

Steroid Conversation

The disclosure that former Raiders defensive lineman Lyle Alzado had been diagnosed with an inoperable brain tumor in 1991 continues to spark conversations about the extent of steroid abuse in the NFL. Alzado, who died on May 14, 1992, said the ailment was caused by his steroid use.

Dan Hampton maintains strong feelings about the subject. "I feel bad for Mr. Alzado. I think that he had to understand that he was doing it to himself. No one was holding a gun on him. I know his motives were to compete and be able to play in the NFL," said Hampton. "That is good and fine. I never took one steroid. I will take a lie-detector test. I didn't have to have it. I'm fortunate, maybe I'm lucky. The bottom line is, for him to indict the entire league as being rampant with steroid use—that is not right of him. Maybe there have been a few players on our team who have done it, but I don't think you will see anything like what he is talking about. I feel bad for him, but I don't think he should paint the rest of the league with the same brush that he has been painted with.

"I used to come to camp and see guys a lot bigger than they were the season before. We would go into Tampa or Pittsburgh and these guys would look like a Volkswagen with shoulder pads on. I think it [steroid testing] is good. It gives everybody the same ground to play on.

"I used to resent the fact that I had to play against guys who were using it. If they want to take the chances with it, that was their decision. Overall, I think the league has done a great job of getting steroids under control or even out of the picture." —F.M.

Surf's Up!

Tom Thayer was one of the dependable offensive linemen on the Super Bowl champion Bears. He has made a successful transition to the broadcast booth as a Bears analyst on WBBM radio in

Chicago, and he has learned the secret to handling the frigid Chicago winters.

Since he retired in 1993, Thayer has been spending about five months a year in Hawaii. He said he always went out there as a player just for a rehabilitation period and to get out of the winters in Chicago. Tom considers himself an active person out in Hawaii and he has really gotten into surfing. He said he wishes Lake Michigan had waves; then he would stay in Chicago all year round. But he has become so infatuated with surfing that it draws him to Hawaii every year.

Surfing the waves in Hawaii is not exactly the same as competing on the football field, but it might be the next best adrenalin rush for Thayer. He says that on Sundays in the NFL as a player, he would get feelings of nervousness, anticipation, excitement, and fear in the pit of his stomach. When he pulls up to the ocean and sees some big waves in Hawaii, the same emotions go through his stomach. He is nervous and excited. It is something that he really has to concentrate on. He loves it because it fills the void that football left when he finished his career. —F.M.

Helping Others

Former Bears stars Jim McMahon and Kevin Butler remain popular and committed when it comes to helping pro football fans worldwide. In 2006, I was pleased to see them step up and lend their services to help cheer up the soldiers overseas. McMahon and Butler flew on Blackhawk helicopters in Iraq to deliver sports apparel to the troops from the Chicago Blackhawks. I thought that was very cool.

McMahon also is actively involved in an annual benefit to raise money and awareness for neuroblastoma, a rare form of pediatric cancer. His golf event, called the "Barefoot Open," was put together after one of McMahon's best friends, Todd Wilkins, and his wife lost their young son, Michael, to that dreaded disease.

"When my boy got sick, Jim really took a personal interest in making sure that our family was okay," Wilkins said.

The Barefoot Open, named after McMahon's penchant for golfing in his bare feet, was held for the first time in 2006 at Geneva National Golf Club in Lake Geneva, Wisconsin. McMahon invited 10 of his friends from sports and entertainment to participate as team captains.

Jim McMahon's penchant for golfing barefoot continues to this day.

"We want to keep it small and exclusive, where people can enjoy getting to know each other and also not lose sight of why we are there," said McMahon. The list of celebrities have included Tom Dreesen, Mark Rypien, Steve McMichael, Brian Noonan, Bernie Nicholls, and Eddie Payton.

"Our goal is to make Neuroblastoma Kids a national organization. We feel if we can raise awareness and dollars for research for neuroblastoma we can help other pediatric cancers as well," McMahon added. —D.J.

chapter 9
Bears Around the World

Olympic Stadium in Berlin, Germany, where 66,876 fans watched the Bears and 49ers in a 1991 preseason game.
(Photo courtesy of Bill Smith)

Topless Overseas

I watched the Bears quickly become an international phenomenon, beginning in 1986 when they took their act overseas to play Dallas in a preseason game in London. In 1988, the Bears faced the Minnesota Vikings in Goteborg, Sweden. And in 1994, the NFL invited the Bears to play the San Francisco 49ers in Berlin, Germany.

The highlight of the trip to Sweden, at least for many of the Bears players, came during the week of practice before the game with the Vikings. The Bears were practicing on a local soccer field when a Swedish model and her camera crew were filming a clothing commercial on the track alongside the soccer field.

In a country that always has been light-years ahead of the United States in terms of sexual expression, the Swedish model thought nothing of changing outfits in full view of everyone in attendance. When she pulled a sweater over her head to change tops, leaving nothing to the imagination, Ditka nearly swallowed his whistle and Bears players froze in their tracks with their mouths wide-open in astonishment. As the model realized she had caused a stir, she quickly covered herself up and the Bears returned to live action on the playing field. —F.M.

Foreign Auditions

"The Turk" traverses oceans and continents, speaks many languages, and often shows up where you least expect him. Rookies in the National Football League, particularly, are painfully aware of the omnipresent "Turk." It's not clear where the moniker originated, but "the Turk" is the team employee designated to tell a player he's been cut. He even made the overseas trip to Sweden; many Bears received the discouraging word following that 1988 exhibition game against the Minnesota Vikings.

"The Turk" never announces his precise itinerary. The Bears, like other NFL teams, had to be down to 60 players by August

23, 1988, and 47 players by August 29. This time, the Bears players who were cut had the opportunity to fly back to the United States with the coaching staff that chose to cut them. —F.M.

America's Game

For the most part, the Swedish fans knew just when to cheer, when to roar, and even when to raise their arms for that nauseating American creation, the Wave, when the Bears faced the Vikings in that 1988 preseason game. A Swedish public address announcer enlightened the nouveau National Football League fans with explanations of the game as the plays unfolded. Now, if only the Bears defense had been prompted to do its part against Minnesota, the Vikings might not have emerged with their 28–21 exhibition victory in the rain at Ullevi Stadium.

A crowd of 33,115 fans bearing signs, placards, and broad smiles seemed thoroughly entertained by the histrionics displayed by the NFC Central Division rivals. "Are all the American football games like this one?" asked one spirited Swedish fan as he departed the stadium. "This was the first football game I've ever seen. It was...different."

For fans accustomed to counting up the score on one foot in their 52,000-seat soccer stadium, the 49-point total certainly was different. —F.M.

German Road Trip

Preparation for the Bears' 1991 season included an overseas trip to Berlin, Germany, to face the San Francisco 49ers. The Bears arrived there wearing their game faces. Mean, ornery, grumpy. Understandably, their bodies were not quite ready for action. Following an eight-hour flight from Chicago, and the seven-hour time difference in Germany, the Bears were put through practice paces by Ditka at majestic Olympic Stadium, where they would play the 49ers later that week. Bears players received 6:00 AM wakeup calls during their stay in Germany, but they would catch a break by having only one practice session a day. They had been practicing twice a day in Platteville, Wisconsin.

Still, it was difficult not to be awed by the new and different surroundings. "The stadium where Jesse Owens won all those gold medals [in 1936] was pretty nice," said receiver Dennis Gentry.

Chris Zorich, a rookie defensive tackle in 1991, thought he had the solution to the jet lag he and his teammates felt. "Throughout my studies at Notre Dame, I found out that if you are going to pull an all-nighter, you have to stay up until the normal time you are supposed to go to bed the next night. Otherwise, your body gets all screwed up," he said. —F.M.

The city of Berlin, Germany, played host to the Bears and 49ers for a preseason game in 1991. (Photo courtesy of Bill Smith)

Ein Bier, Bitte

While German fans were learning how to say "Da Bears," the players were issued a list of commonly used phrases to help them get along during the week of preparation for the preseason contest against the San Francisco 49ers. A few examples:

—"Ein Bier, bitte" translates to "One beer, please."
—"Wo ist die Toilette?" means "Where is the toilet?"
—"Wo kann ich die Polizei finden?" means "Where can I find a policeman?"

But no translation was necessary after the Bears' charter flight arrived in Berlin. Ditka immediately put his players through practice. Ditka agreed to have his players work with the 49ers, as long as they were willing to get up and work at the time the Bears were up. Otherwise, the Bears planned to work by themselves. Wakeup call was at 6:00 AM , and rookies had their ankles taped and then ate breakfast from 6:15 to 7:15 AM. Veterans ate from 7:15 to 8:15 AM. After team meetings, practices were conducted from 10:45 AM to 1:00 PM. After that extensive regimen, there was little time to ask for, "One beer, please." —D.J.

chapter 10
The Wannstedt Era

Dave Wannstedt succeeded Mike Ditka as head coach of the Bears in 1993. He was fired six seasons later after leading the team to only one postseason appearance.
(Photo courtesy of Bill Smith)

Staying in Communication

NFL experts are divided when it comes to assessing the head coaching ability of Dave Wannstedt. But I found the former Bears coach to be warm and engaging off the field, with tremendous family values. As much of a workaholic as he is, Wannstedt was able to enjoy quality time at home with his family, which includes daughters Keri and Jami, who were teenagers when he coached the Bears in the 1990s. Wannstedt, now the head coach at his alma mater, Pittsburgh, had developed a reputation for being a players' coach with excellent motivational skills. That seemed to be the way he handled his situation at home, too. At least that is what his wife, Jan, said.

She told me that her husband had been pretty consistent throughout the years as he tried to balance his demanding career and family life. Jan said the roller-coaster ride of coaching can be at once very tough and a great deal of fun. Dave did a good job of separating his personal and professional life. As a college assistant coach, he would call every day to touch base with his kids when he was on the road recruiting. He would call to tell the kids goodnight or he would call in the morning to tell them to have a good day at school. That was something that was really important to him.

Wannstedt maintained a family-type atmosphere with his Bears coaching staff. Most of them jogged together daily, a tradition carried over from Dave's days with the Dallas Cowboys. When his second training camp with the Bears opened, Wannstedt tried to emphasize open communication among his players. During Wannstedt's first summer camp, wide receiver Curtis Conway spoke out about the strenuous two-a-day work-outs, before the Bears went on to finish a disappointing 7–9 regular season.

"That cropped up on day one or two," veteran offensive tackle Andy Heck recalled. "I think that could have been possibly blown out of proportion a little bit. I mean, Curtis made a comment and everybody jumped all over it. But Curtis works as hard as anybody and likes to work as hard as anybody.

"Dave responded to that criticism with open arms and open communication. He proved that he is willing to have dialogue with players. He had a committee of guys meet with him once a week to talk about those kinds of things. I think the communication has always been good. Maybe guys didn't realize it and then they voiced some concerns.

"Dave said, 'What are your concerns? If you have them, you don't have to announce them in the papers. You can come right to me.' I thought he was great about that." —F.M.

Running Buddies

For 15 years, former Cowboys coach Jimmy Johnson and Wannstedt were running buddies. They coached together at the University of Pittsburgh, Oklahoma State, Miami, and finally, Dallas. Johnson, Wannstedt, and the rest of the coaching staff would participate in daily jogs. They found it to be an informal way of brainstorming coaching ideas for the team.

But those jogging sessions between the two coaches had to come to an end when Wannstedt took over as head coach of the Bears. Although Wannstedt continued to regularly speak to Johnson on the phone, he was trying to prove he could coach well on his own. Wannstedt's wife, Jan, felt it was time for Wannstedt to become more of his own man. Dave previously had left Oklahoma State to coach at USC—without Johnson, for a change. Jan Wannstedt called her husband's decision to accept a position at USC "the best move we made" because it was the first time they had ventured off on their own. She said it was a "real growing time for us."

The Johnson/Wannstedt relationship facilitated the trade between the Bears and Cowboys that sent linebackers Vinson Smith and Barry Minter and a sixth-round 1995 draft pick to the Bears for tight end Kelly Blackwell, safety Markus Paul, and linebacker John Roper.

"There is no question that helped the trade," said Johnson. "Number one, I wouldn't have traded Vinson Smith to another team [other than the Bears]. I know Dave's relationship with Vinson and that Vinson had a strong feeling for Dave. So he would accept playing in Chicago. That was one factor."

The trade was Johnson's 49th since taking over as Cowboys coach. Smith played well for the Bears, and Minter contributed on special teams. Meanwhile, the Cowboys wound up releasing Blackwell, Paul, and Roper. Blackwell signed with the Rams before the last game of that season. Roper was picked up by the Eagles. Paul re-signed with the Bears before being released again and signing with Tampa Bay. —F.M.

Cover Boy

Whether he wanted to or not, Dave Wannstedt would share much of the glory or blame for the 1994 season with Bears president Michael McCaskey, who chose to have his picture on the cover of the media guide with the new coach.

Dave Wannstedt and team president Michael McCaskey toured Soldier Field after Wannstedt was named head coach in 1993.

Unlike the rocky relationship between Ditka and McCaskey, Wannstedt was determined to make this new partnership work. Wannstedt took advantage of McCaskey's open-door policy and often stopped by his office to chat about football or other topics. Wannstedt said he would take a cup of coffee and walk down the hall and just sit down and talk about the guys in the weight room. Or McCaskey would come in and talk about one of the changes in the new bargaining agreement or something like that. They got along fine. In fact, when Wannstedt had three years remaining on his contract with the Bears, McCaskey had to put to rest rumors that his coach would be the next field boss of the Dallas Cowboys.

Cowboys owner Jerry Jones would have had to obtain official permission from the Bears to talk to Wannstedt. Jones, in San Diego for the Super Bowl, did not rule out the possibility of seeking permission from the Bears to talk to the former Dallas defensive coordinator. Several Cowboys players, including quarterback Troy Aikman, had said they would be in favor of having Wannstedt take over for Barry Switzer, who resigned under pressure.

"Let's put a stop to those rumors right now, because we have got the stopper," McCaskey said of the Bears' right of refusal.

Asked if the Cowboys had sought permission to negotiate with Wannstedt, McCaskey replied succinctly: "Dave Wannstedt is going to be the coach of the Chicago Bears next year. Period. End of story." —F.M.

A Real Kick

As a rookie, Todd Sauerbrun was hazed by some veteran Bears players in 1995 when he showed up at training camp driving a fancy sports car with a vanity plate that read "Hang Time." They shaved his head and taunted him repeatedly. Sauerbrun now calls those veterans "the worst group of guys I have ever been around. Bad people. Vindictive and mean-spirited. I'd like to see them try to do that to me now."

Sauerbrun often clashed with former Bears special teams coach Keith Armstrong. He claimed the Bears often wanted him to punt 35 yards toward the sideline. Sauerbrun was a second-round draft pick out of West Virginia, where he set an NCAA record with a career gross punting average of 46.3 yards, and he said he is not comfortable directional kicking. He calls himself a "big-hit punter." He said, "That's like telling Frank Thomas to just go hit singles. And to tell Sammy Sosa, 'Come on, we just need you to get on base.' Are you going to do that? I don't think so."

During his five-year tenure with the Bears, Sauerbrun often caught the brunt of criticism from head coach Dave Wannstedt, even though many of those teams were deficient in several other key areas. Sauerbrun describes the instruction he received from the Bears as "overcoaching from people who didn't know what they were talking about. I did not have a good time there. I did not enjoy myself. Chicago is a great city; I love Chicago. But it just

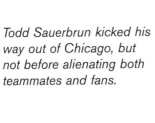

Todd Sauerbrun kicked his way out of Chicago, but not before alienating both teammates and fans.

didn't work out for me over there. I definitely needed to get out of there. That [leaving the Bears] was the best thing that could have ever happened to me."

He also criticized the Chicago Park District for failing to properly maintain the Soldier Field playing surface during his stint with the Bears. "It was embarrassing," he said.

Sauerbrun signed with Kansas City as a free agent in 2000, joined Carolina the following year, and kicked for Denver in 2005 and 2007 before being cut toward the end of the season, perhaps due in part to a series of off-the-field issues. "I would never do anything different in my life. I went through life saying to myself, *I will not regret anything that I do*," he said. "I will enjoy my life to the fullest, and that is the way I am going to live. No regrets."

Asked whether there would be any way he would return to the Bears later in his career as a free agent, Sauerbrun replied, "If they overpaid me, yeah. I would love the Bears."

The Bears provided Sauerbrun one of the worst memories of his career in November 2007, when his Denver Broncos came to Chicago. Sauerbrun had provided tickets for 40 friends and family members to watch him experience a kicker's worst nightmare at Soldier Field.

Sauerbrun had boasted the previous week that his team did not fear Bears Pro Bowl kick returner Devin Hester. Yet Sauerbrun had one of his punts returned 75 yards for a touchdown by Hester, and then Hester returned a kickoff 88 yards for another score. To really make his day, Charles Tillman blocked one of Sauerbrun's punt attempts to set up a Bears touchdown by Adrian Peterson.

"Isn't that nice? Forty people to come see this stinkin' mess," said Sauerbrun, who still owns a home in Chicago. "That was the craziest game I have ever been involved in in my life. I had the trifecta done to me today."

Hester became the 10th player in NFL history with two kick-return touchdowns in the same quarter. "I think I'm going to sell my house now," Sauerbrun joked. "But all props to Devin. The guy belongs in the Pro Bowl."

Sauerbrun, who earned Pro Bowl selections in 2001, 2002, and 2003 after leaving the Bears, watched a 34–20 fourth-quarter lead vanish as Denver lost 37–34 to the Bears in overtime.

"The field [stinks], the game [stinks], the weather [stinks]. But so what. They had to deal with it, too," said Sauerbrun. "It was not a pleasurable day all around, regardless of anything. They kicked our ass, plain and simple."

Sauerbrun, generally considered a capable tackler, twice whiffed on Hester as the last man with a decent shot to stop him. "That field is slippery as heck, and you give him room...with that much room in between us...I don't really have a chance," said Sauerbrun, who was a high school All-American lacrosse player. "You have to poke and hope. Mostly hope."

"Today was just an extremely bad day." —F.M.

A Hat on a Hat

When it comes to violent, helmet-to-helmet player collisions, the bloodied face and contorted lower leg of former Bears wide receiver Tom Waddle flashes across my mental screen.

"Basically, it was the beginning of the end of my career," says Waddle of the 1994 hit laid on him by Tampa Bay defensive back Thomas Everett. "I had several stitches in my face, I partially tore a knee ligament, I reinjured a hip. I think my career was kind of coming to an end anyway, but [the hit] certainly sped it up. I mean, there are just certain injuries that some guys can come back from. But cumulatively, when you add them all up for me, it was just too much."

The NFL has cracked down on helmet-to-helmet hits in recent years, levying stiff fines and suspensions for such indiscretions. Yet Waddle holds no bitterness toward the way the game was officiated when he played. "The last thing I would have ever done would be to whine about how hard a guy hit me, with his helmet or without. I don't think the players have as much of an issue with it as the league does at this point," he said.

Wide receiver Tom Waddle was a fan favorite lauded for his ability to make tough catches across the middle of the field. (Photo courtesy of Bill Smith)

"You let the referees take care of it. You just accept the hit, knowing that is part of being a football player. But I was a little surprised that Thomas Everett wasn't flagged. I wasn't angry at Thomas Everett. I understood that was my role. But I was a little surprised that when a guy leads with his head and goes head-to-head...the rule specifically says that's illegal. You gotta follow the rules."

Now a member of the sports media, Waddle also understands the hypocrisy of the NFL promoting the violent nature of the game in its advertising. "It is a violent game, and when you add the competitiveness of the NFC North Division, that adds to it," said Waddle. "The NFL is a media creature. We are all used to the big hits, the home run, the car wreck. That's what people want to see." —F.M.

The Tight End Buzz

When the Bears selected tight end Greg Olsen from the University of Miami in 2007, it was the first time the franchise had selected a tight end in the first round since Mike Ditka was taken out of Pittsburgh in 1961. Olsen augments a position that was already receiving improved production from veteran Desmond Clark in 2006.

Before those two arrived, there had been a pox on the Bears' tight end position for more than two decades. Since Emery Moorehead starred for the Super Bowl XX champions in the 1980s, there had been an injury hex on Bears tight ends like nobody's business. Moorehead retired after the 1988 season relatively unscathed. Before Moorehead, Ditka gave the position stature and definition in the 1960s, and he later became the first tight end to be inducted into the Pro Football Hall of Fame. Greg Latta also had some productive years in the '70s. But injuries ranging from the simply nagging to the career-threatening became the norm when the position was taken over by the likes of Tim Wrightman, Cap Boso, James "Robocop" Thornton, Chris Gedney, Marv Cook, Keith Jennings, Ryan Wetnight, Bobby Neely, and John Allred.

"Tight end was a difficult position and it was not the players' faults," said former Bears coach Dave Wannstedt about the excessive injuries.

Allred had 54 catches for 589 yards with three touchdowns at Southern Cal. The 6'4", 246-pounder played in both the Cotton and Rose Bowls. Allred broke his left leg late in the 1993 season, returned to start three games the next season, and then broke it again in practice.

James Coley, a Bears backup tight end several years ago, suffered the most unlikely and ignominious setback. He was stung by a bee when it flew up his nose during practice behind Halas Hall in Lake Forest in 1990. He had to be rushed to the hospital because his throat and nasal passages began to swell.

John Allred was one of many tight ends the Bears have drafted who failed to make an impact on the field.

Many players suffer numbing nerve injuries in the shoulder and neck area commonly called "stingers," but Coley's stinger was the buzz around the Bears locker room for weeks afterward.

Coley was the first Bears player in 11 years at Halas Hall to be stung by a bee. Later that same season, a coach also was stung. It was, of course, the tight ends coach, Steve Kazor. The good-natured Coley was able to smile about the uncomfortable occurrence the next day, telling me and other reporters that it would take more than a bee sting in his nose to stop him.

Boso's career ended prematurely in 1992 following the last of several knee surgeries. Wrightman played for only two years before attempting a less physically intimidating career as a standup comedian. Thornton, who later signed a $1 million free-agent contract with the Jets, never fulfilled his potential with the Bears because of a file full of medical problems. The most devastating: a torn plantar fascia tendon in his left foot.

Gedney, a 6'5", 265 pound third-round draft pick from Syracuse in 1993, missed half of his rookie season with a broken collar bone and the same torn plantar fascia tendon in his left foot that rendered Thornton unavailable.

Before joining the Bears, Cook, a former two-time Pro Bowl tight end with New England, had never missed an NFL regular-season game. But guess what? Cook came to the Bears and injured his back during a noncontact minicamp. He was unable to play in the first two preseason games and never returned to top form.

"I had a stress fracture in my foot when I was a rookie and I missed about three weeks of training camp," said Cook when asked to recall any other time an injury kept him from his appointed rounds.

Cook wore a red jersey with a white cross on his back during workouts immediately after suffering his back injury. "It was just the trainer's way of making sure no one hit me," Cook recalls. Perhaps the Bears should have all of their tight ends wear a red jersey during games. Anything to end the position's long-standing injury hex. —F.M.

Live and Learn

Linebacker Bryan Cox was renowned for his temper tantrums that drew record fines from the NFL during his short stint with the Bears. The Bears were a combined 11–21 in 1996–97 under Wannstedt, and Cox recalled his frustration during that period.

"Those were some of the lowest times I had because I felt like I was playing for an organization that wasn't trying to win," said Cox.

Cox, who signed as a free agent with the Patriots after being released by the Bears and later the New York Jets, tried to repress his memories of playing for the Bears organization. "I don't think this is the appropriate spot to take cheap shots or talk negatively about anybody," said Cox. "I am here, I am happy. The Bears are where they are and I am not going to belittle myself or them. That's not right."

Linebacker Bryan Cox was signed as a free agent in 1996; he played just two seasons for the Bears before moving on to the New York Jets. (Photo courtesy of Bill Smith)

Cox, who now spends more time reading the Bible, praised former Jets coach Bill Parcells for helping him develop as an individual. "Playing for him [Parcells], I was able to mature," said Cox. "I was able to learn from him. When I was going through a divorce I was able to talk to him and he was able to kind of walk me through some things. He has been like one of my best friends, yet he has taught me so much. Going to New York may have been the greatest thing that ever happened in my football career, other than being drafted by [former Dolphins coach] Don Shula in 1991."

Cox was one of several questionable personnel moves during the Wannstedt era. Rashaan Salaam never became the running back the Bears hoped he would be, and the acquisition of quarterback Rick Mirer also turned out to be a bust. The former Notre Dame quarterback and first-round draft pick was acquired from Seattle in exchange for a Bears number one draft pick, but Mirer was unable to reverse the trend of poor quarterback play. UCLA's Cade McNown was another first-round draft choice at quarterback for the Bears. His brief career was marked by poor leadership skills and work habits. —F.M.

Bear Weather?

The myth of "Bear weather" seemed to be emphatically debunked on January 8, 1989, when Joe Montana and the San Francisco 49ers skated past the Bears 28–3 in the NFC Championship Game at Soldier Field in frigid temperatures. Since that deep-freezing defeat, the Bears have continued to falter in games played in December and January.

In 1993, Dave Wannstedt's first year as head coach, the Bears finished 7–9 and in fourth place in the NFC Central Division. They were 7–5 and in prime position to secure a playoff spot entering the middle of December, but a four-game losing streak at the end of the year kept the Bears at home. "Our number one goal [in 1994] will be to win games in December," Wannstedt said following his first season. "I guarantee that we will find a way to win in December."

The Bears managed to go just 1–3 in December of '94, which gave them a 9–7 record and a NFC Wild Card berth. The Bears beat the Vikings 35–18 on New Year's Day at the Metrodome before being clobbered 44–15 by the 49ers in San Francisco.

Current Bears coach Lovie Smith says he looks forward to frigid temperatures at Soldier Field. "That's our home-field advantage. The colder the better," Smith says. —D.J.

The "Next Payton" Goes Up in Smoke

A series of ill-fated drafts during the Dave Wannstedt era included the selection of Heisman Trophy–winning running back Rashaan Salaam out of Colorado in 1995. Rashaan Iman Salaam appeared to be a determined young man with great expectations. Foremost, there were the high expectations and stringent guidelines set by his parents, who wanted him to become a more devoted Muslim and a solid, contributing adult. Second, there were the grand expectations of the Bears, who drafted the 20-year-old running back in the first round and wanted desperately for him to become the answer to their blossoming running game. And, perhaps most important, there were the lofty long-range expectations of Salaam himself to successfully perpetuate the Bears' proud tradition of dominant running backs.

Salaam saw himself becoming the Bears' next Walter Payton, strong, durable, and dependable. Payton, the NFL's all-time leading rusher when he retired, even telephoned Salaam right after the draft to impart his wisdom. "He just called me and gave me encouragement," said Salaam. "He said that when I saw him he would have a packet of his workout programs for me. He is a busy man and he is enjoying life like he should. That is what I want to be like after 13 years in Chicago." But Salaam fumbled Payton's advice.

After an encouraging rookie season with the Bears during which Salaam gained 1,074 yards, his playing career and personal life began spiraling downhill. His penchant for fumbling in key situations, coupled with injuries, reduced the team's faith in him. He rushed for only 496 yards in 1996 as he split time with Raymont Harris in the backfield. In '97, he gained 112 yards on the season. And then he was gone from the Bears.

Salaam played briefly in the short-lived XFL before bruising a shoulder and missing several games. "I loved it, though. I got a chance to get my confidence back," he said. But a tryout with the Detroit Lions did not earn him a spot on the roster, and Salaam realized the sand in his NFL hourglass was running out.

Former Heisman Trophy winner Rashaan Salaam lasted just three disappointing seasons in Chicago.

"I mean, to go in the first round, you win the Heisman, everything happens in just a big whirlwind," said Salaam. "Now I appreciate the game and I really appreciate the work you have got to put into it. You have to take care of your body 24/7. There is no off-season. I understand that it is really a business."

He later second-guessed his decision to leave Colorado after winning the Heisman in his junior season. "Staying in college another year would have helped me a lot," said Salaam. "I was so young age-wise. I didn't see how hard it is to get there. I mean I worked and everything, but I kind of got through things kind of easy. I took life for granted. If I had taken my workout regimen more seriously and if I had been more accessible to the fans…. The fans were behind me all the time."

Salaam also realized that his college success was not a passport through the NFL. "Winning the Heisman wasn't a curse," said Salaam. "I sort of made it that way. I had a gift and I abused my gift. I didn't respect the game. When I won the Heisman, all of that stuff probably went to my head. I thought it was going to be a cakewalk. I didn't realize there were going to be potholes there."

After departing the Bears, Salaam admitted he had become obsessed with smoking marijuana as his professional football career was spinning out of control. That's where the storybook tale began to unravel, or more accurately, go up in smoke. "It really took the life out of me. It took away my love for football. My love turned toward the weed," said Salaam. "That's not the person I really am, you know what I'm saying. I want to play football, not smoke weed all my life. My life got away from me. It was like my Kryptonite." —F.M.

chapter 11
The Cheeseheads

Steve McMichael is one of many players who played for both the Bears and rival Packers.

Pouring It On

During my tenure with the Bears, I was able to enjoy the most lop-sided victory in the storied history of the Bears-Packers rivalry. In 1980, we walloped Green Bay 61–7. Everything we did that day seemed to work. Well, actually we had two extra points misfire, so the score could have been an even more imposing 63–7. We finished with a 7–9 record in 1980 and the Packers were 5–10–1, so neither one of us was exactly headed to the playoffs that year. But we did exact a measure of revenge in destroying our rivals from the north.

Interestingly, we lost the first game against the Packers that season by the score of 12–6 in Green Bay. That contest was bizarre in another sense. We were tied 6–6 going into overtime at Lambeau Field. But Lynn Dickey threw a 32-yard pass to James Lofton to set up a possible game-winning field goal by Chester Marcol. But Marcol's kick was blocked by Alan Page. The ball sailed up in the air and into the arms of Marcol, who shockingly was able to run it in for the winning touchdown.

Lee Remmel, the Packers' revered historian, has witnessed 124 of the 175 Bears-Packers contests. Remmel says the rivalry has seen each team go through some lean years while the other club was doing exceptionally well. And, of course, some years both teams have played well. Interestingly, the all-time record has remained fairly balanced: the Bears have the edge 90–79–6.

A sportswriter with the *Green Bay Post Gazette* for 25 years before joining the Packers organization in 1974, Remmel formed strong relationships with both Bears founder George Halas and Packers coaching icon Vince Lombardi. He recalled that Halas needed money to meet his player payroll in the 1930s and went to the Packers for a $1,500 loan.

Remmel also remembers hearing Lombardi saying, "Papa George, I love that man." He says there was a great mutual admiration between the two NFL pioneers. On the other side of the coin, Vince couldn't stand Curly Lambeau, the founder of the Packers. He had nothing good to say about him. But he loved George Halas. —D.J.

Bears in Packers' Clothing

As far as can be determined, there is no debriefing, no brainwashing, no intense interrogation room where players are forced to renounce their former allegiance under the glare of unbearably bright lights. But clearly something peculiar happens when a Bears player changes uniforms and becomes (gasp!) a Green Bay Packer. One of the most storied rivalries in all of pro sports sometimes challenges the loyalty of the combatants who change enemy lines.

"When I cleaned out my Bears locker, I kept my defensive playbook and I gave it to [then Packers coach] Mike Holmgren when I got up there. All is fair in love and war, baby," confessed Steve McMichael, who spent 13 seasons toiling for the Bears (1981–93) and despising the Packers before signing a contract with Green Bay for his final season. "I stole money by signing with the Packers," McMichael now says with a laugh.

Bears Super Bowl quarterback Jim McMahon ultimately defected to Green Bay. So did Mike Tomczak. Linebacker Jim Morrissey swallowed his pride and played for the Packers after performing well for the Bears from 1985 to 1993. Wide receiver Anthony Morgan couldn't get out of Dave Wannstedt's doghouse with the Bears, so he signed with Green Bay and played there from 1993 to 1996.

Former Bears running back Edgar Bennett not only began his career with the Packers, but also went to work in Green Bay's front office after his playing days were over. In decades past, Bears backup quarterback Zeke Bratkowski found money and opportunity in Green Bay after playing for the Bears in 1954 and from 1957 to 1960. He played for the Packers from 1963 to 1968, and then again in 1971.

Jim Flanigan played in 108 games over his seven seasons with the Bears, starting 88 games, before he joined the Packers. "Within a day or two, I was accepted by my [Packers] teammates, and I felt very comfortable here," says Flanigan, who was a salary cap casualty of the Bears. "Our defensive scheme was similar to what we did on the Bears with Dave Wannstedt. So, in that regard, I fit right in. Within a day or two I felt like I knew what I was doing. They did a good job of welcoming me."

Flanigan's father, Jim, was a second-round selection in Green Bay's 1967 draft as a linebacker. It was the last draft conducted by the late Vince Lombardi as head coach of the Packers.

Former Bears coach George Halas used to threaten his players by saying he would trade them to Green Bay—the NFL's version of Siberia at the time, the Packers went 12 years without a winning season in the late '40s and '50s—if they didn't perform better on the field. Those were the days when the Packers were struggling before the arrival of Lombardi, and the prospect of leaving the more glamorous metropolis of Chicago for tiny Green Bay, Wisconsin, carried some weight.

Many former Bears players had no choice but to head north. "I want all of the fans to get it straight," said McMichael, who set the Bears record for consecutive games played—191—as a defensive tackle. "The Bears cut me and Green Bay called me with some money. That's why I went up there. It was business.

"I went up there and was welcomed with open arms in that locker room. I got respect from the players, and even the fans. When I would walk around Green Bay...they all knew I came from the Bears. They hated me for 13 years [while he was a Bear], but they accepted me there with open arms. They would say, 'Oh, you play for *us* now and you can help us beat the Bears.'"

McMahon, who also had brief stops in Cleveland and Minnesota after starring for the Bears, says he felt no pangs of guilt in Green Bay, either. "When I was with the Packers (1995–96), playing the Bears was not really a big deal," he said. "The rivalry was still there, certainly, but the bad blood was pretty much gone as far as the cheap shots and trying to hurt people on almost every play. That's how it was when I was with the Bears playing them. Plus, the Bears were awful then, so other than it being Bears-Packers week, there really wasn't a lot of bad blood."

McMahon was a victim of one of those cheap shots when former Packers defender Charles Martin leveled him with a blind-side hit several seconds after McMahon had released a pass. Martin, who had McMahon's name on a "hit list" on a towel tucked inside his uniform, was immediately ejected from the game.

Those were the years when Bears coach Mike Ditka and Packers coach Forrest Gregg—both Hall of Fame players—let their personal disdain for each other get in the way of good sportsmanship. Gregg allegedly ordered many of the cheap shots on Bears players. "That's how it all started—Forrest and Mike didn't like each other," said McMahon. "They still don't. It started with them and trickled down to everyone else. They probably took the game more personally than we did."

Packer fans took the game personally then, too. McMahon remembers the blistering comments coming from the stands that are so close to the field at Lambeau. "You yell back and press on," said McMahon. "Back then, all they could do was yell, because the Packers couldn't play."

Tomczak was a member of the 4–12 Packers team in 1991, playing behind starting quarterback Don Majkowski. When the Packers acquired Brett Favre in a trade with Atlanta in 1992, Tomczak was released in training camp. "The fans were tremendous up there in Green Bay," said Tomczak, who is now a sports broadcaster. "It was similar to the Bears fans. It was a lot different setting. It is obviously a smaller town but they were very rabid. When I came back with the Packers to play the Bears in '91, a lot of the Cheesehead loyalists traveled down to Chicago. It is one of the greatest rivalries of all, regardless of whether you are playing for Chicago or Green Bay. It is still *the* game."

Tomczak, who also played for Pittsburgh, Cleveland, and Detroit before retiring, tried to think of a rivalry that compares to the Bears and Packers. "Pittsburgh against Cleveland," he said. "One thing about my career, I played for organizations that were real rich in traditions—Green Bay, Chicago, Pittsburgh, Cleveland, and Detroit. I would say the Pittsburgh-Cleveland rivalry was the best from the standpoint of being similar towns."

Simply wearing a Packers uniform does not transform an original Bears player. "I always will be a Bear," said McMichael. "I was drafted by the New England Patriots and run out of there after my rookie year. Then George Halas signed me to my first contract. I was kind of blackballed from the league because I was a wild child in practice and in my private life. [Former Patriots coaches] Ron Erhardt and Fritz Shurmur, on the day they cut me they told me, 'We think you are the criminal element in the league.' But that's what George Halas was. In other words, I would probably be working in the oil fields if it wasn't for George Halas and the Chicago Bears. The 13 years that I played here were my heart, my pride. New England and Green Bay were just business. It doesn't matter where you travel and where you pitch your tent. Where your heart is...that's where you come back to. And I will always be a Monster of the Midway, baby." —D.J.

Turn-Down Service

The Bears made no attempt to sign Reggie White when he was the NFL's most sought-after free agent in 1993. Instead, the Bears and new coach Dave Wannstedt put their faith in Alonzo Spellman, who wound up with a paltry 2.5 sacks that year. The Bears lost their final four games to finish 7–9 and miss the play-offs in '93. White, who passed away in 2004 at the age of 43, surprised most observers by accepting a four-year, $17 million offer from the Packers. He wound up his career as the NFL's all-time leader in quarterback sacks, a mark later eclipsed by Bruce Smith. White and a guy named Brett Favre were key reasons the Packers dominated the Bears throughout much of the decade.

In fact, I remember that White and Favre enjoyed great rapport off the field when they were Packers teammates. White once told me this humorous anecdote: "One time, we were in Chicago doing a commercial and he [Favre] called my room in a woman's voice, asking did I need my bed turned down. Of course, I said no, and he asked then if I wanted him to come up and give me a kiss. I said no—of course. Then I realized it was him. Yes, Brett has played a lot of jokes on me." —F.M.

The Book on Favre

In September 2007 I had an opportunity to talk to Deanna Favre, wife of Packers quarterback Brett Favre, after she wrote a revealing new book titled *Don't Bet Against Me*. In the book she wrote about her personal battle with breast cancer, as well as Brett's well-publicized past addiction to painkillers. Deanna said the book was difficult for her to write because she has always been a very private person. But she realizes that because she is battling breast cancer, it is important for her to get the message out to the many other women fighting the same horrible disease. She also discusses in great detail what she and Brett had to endure while Brett went through his addictions.

In the book, Deanna writes about her husband's excessive drinking and abuse of Vicodin that caused tension in their relationship. So how did Brett feel about her airing the intimate details of their personal problems?

"He was pretty good with it," Deanna told me. She said she had him read everything that was said in the book. She told him, "We can keep it in or we can take it out." It was hard for him to read, says Deanna, but he thought that maybe someone else could read it and benefit from it.

Deanna described Brett as "an awesome person when I met him. He was a lot like me at first, kind of quiet and shy and he really didn't care for the spotlight. What better way to hide than to take a few pills, right? I kind of think that is what happened. He has come a long way." —F.M.

Friendly Rivals

The history of the NFL is replete with examples of club owners and coaches arguing and bickering. But I know that the Bears, owned by the McCaskey family, have maintained a friendly and cordial relationship with Seattle Seahawks coach Mike Holmgren, even when he guided the rival Green Bay Packers. Virginia McCaskey, the daughter of former Bears founder and coach George Halas, presented Holmgren with the NFC championship trophy at Lambeau Field when he coached the Packers. Brian McCaskey, one of Virginia's sons and a longtime executive with the Bears, is a graduate of North Park University in Chicago as is his wife, Barb. North Park is where the relationship between the McCaskeys and Holmgrens got started: Holmgren's wife, Kathy, and their four daughters all attended the school as well.

"Mike and his wife have been very generous with North Park," said Brian, now the Bears senior director of development. The Holmgren athletic facility at the university is state of the art.

"It is kind of neat that two NFL teams have ties to North Park," Brian noted. —D.J.

chapter 12
The Modern Bears

Devin Hester's touchdown return on the opening kickoff of Super Bowl XLI was the highlight of a losing effort.

Weather or Not

I played in some pretty rotten weather conditions during my playing days, including the snow-bound final game of the 1977 season against the New York Giants that Bob Thomas won for us with an overtime field goal to catapult us into the playoffs.

That was such a pivotal victory for the Bears organization, as we finished the '77 season with a 9–5 record. Bob Avellini and Mike Phipps were our quarterbacks. Walter Payton had one of his typical outstanding seasons. And players such as Bo Rather, James Scott, Roland Harper, Brian Baschnagel, Robin Earl, and Greg Latta came through for us offensively.

On defense, playmakers such as Virgil Livers, Doug Plank, Doug Buffone, Mike Hartenstine, Allan Ellis, and Gary Fencik were big contributors for head coach Jack Pardee. Unfortunately for us, Pardee took the head coaching job with the Washington Redskins in 1978 after they offered him a ton of money.

But I have also witnessed some Bears games as a broadcaster that featured snow, wind, rain, and extreme cold. The 1994 Halloween night game between the Bears and Packers at Soldier Field was played in some of the most miserable weather I have ever seen. The rain and sleet was swirling through gusts of wind. That was the night the Bears decided to retire the numbers of Hall of Famers Gale Sayers and Dick Butkus during a halftime ceremony.

Bears offensive coordinator Ron Turner remembered it was so bad that Mark Bortz, who's one of the toughest guys of all time, went to the heater on the sideline to get warm. Bortz said that was the only time in his career he ever did that. And Erik Kramer came in after warm-ups and said to Turner, "Don't call a pass. I can't throw anything."

To make matters worse for Bears fans that night, the Packers routed Chicago in the Monday night contest. But as bad as the weather was that night, the December 23, 2007, game between the Bears and Packers was no bargain, either. A combination of wind and cold made Brett Favre say afterward that it was the worst weather he had ever played in.

The Bears demolished the Packers 35–7 on December 23, 2007, one of the coldest days in the rivalry's history.

The Bears trounced the Packers 35–7 to complete a sweep of the NFC North Division champions. Favre said he had played in colder actual temperatures, but in the 16 years he spent in Green Bay, he learned that wind means everything. It can be zero degrees, and if it's not windy at all, it's a lot easier to manage than 40-mph winds. —D.J.

Just a Bit Outside

Because of the wind that was gusting at 38 miles an hour during a 2005 game against the San Francisco 49ers, the Bears had replacement goal posts set aside underneath the Soldier Field stands to use in case the ones on the field were uprooted and damaged.

Bears kicker Robbie Gould appeared to be aiming for those replacement goal posts stored under the southwest section of the stadium when his 39-yard field-goal attempt began drifting, then drifted even farther away from his intended target—about half the width of a football field wide.

"It wasn't a kicker's paradise out here today; it was a little rough," said Gould, who later connected on a key 37-yard field goal in the fourth quarter to help the Bears beat the 49ers 17–9. "It feels good to get at least one under my belt."

Gould, then a rookie out of Penn State, could hardly believe how badly he missed his first field-goal try because of the wind. "I put it right where I wanted to. It is tough to say you are happy with a miss, but I am happy because I put it exactly where I wanted it and that's where it went. In those conditions that's all you can really do," Gould said.

Bears long snapper Patrick Mannelly, recognized as one of the best in the NFL, even had trouble directing his snaps to kick holder Brad Maynard. "The biggest problem was the gusts," said Mannelly. "If you play in a game with wind, you can kind of play the wind. We would run out there and it would be windy, but all of a sudden it would start gusting. That's the difficult part."

Gould proved his ability in 2006 when he made the NFC Pro Bowl team. —F.M.

Crown 'Em!

When it comes to coaches blowing their top after a tough loss, the Arizona Cardinals' Dennis Green spared no emotion when he erupted after his team blew a 20-point halftime lead to the Bears on *Monday Night Football* in 2006.

The beleaguered Green angrily pounded the podium during his postgame press conference when asked about the then-undefeated Bears, whom the Cardinals had beaten 23–16 in the third game of that preseason.

"The Bears are what we thought they were," Green began. "They are what we thought they were! We played them in preseason. Who the hell picks a third game in preseason like it's meaningless? We played them in the third game. Everybody played three quarters. The Bears are who we thought they were! That's why we took the damn field. If you want to crown them, then crown their ass! They are who we thought they were and we let them off of the hook."

With that, Green stormed out of the room and the Cardinals were left to deal with their fifth straight loss. It was a beautiful thing for Bears fans. Excerpts of Green's now famous rant can be seen in a beer commercial. At least Green gets paid every time it airs now. —D.J.

Don't Touch the Cars

Several years ago, R.W. McQuarters received a huge payday—five years, $21.25 million—so the former Bears cornerback decided to look into buying the car of his dreams. "I have a car fetish. I really have a car fetish," McQuarters admits now. "The Ferrari is something I have been wanting for a long time. I was just going in to look."

McQuarters, now a member of the Super Bowl XLII champion New York Giants, and a friend took a ride over to the nearby Lake Forest Sports Cars dealership. That's where an incident of conflicting reports took place. McQuarters said he and his friend "from back home in Oklahoma," both dressed in blue jeans, T-shirts, and tennis shoes, were disrespected by the salesperson after they attempted to look inside one of the showroom cars.

"I didn't know you weren't supposed to touch the cars. There is not a sign up there that says, 'Don't touch the cars' or nothing," said McQuarters. "But the guy was saying, 'Don't touch the cars.' So I looked at the guy and said, 'Isn't that the business you're in? If somebody comes in looking for a car and they happen to touch it...somebody is going to touch the car. You just wipe it off at the end of the day.'

"He said, 'No, that's not the business I'm in. I'm into selling cars.' Then he got smart. On my way out I said, 'If anybody asks,

R.W. McQuarters's love for sports cars led to a disagreement with a Lake Forest car dealership.

I'm R.W. McQuarters of the Bears who came by and I will be sure not to send anybody else over here.'"

Rick Mancuso, president of Lake Forest Sports Cars, told a Chicago radio station that he characterized the atmosphere as threatening when McQuarters and his friend entered the dealership. "More from his buddy," said Mancuso. "I think he [McQuarters] stayed reasonably calm. I didn't hear him say much. The [friend] was so loud, that's all we could hear. I can't tell you how far out of the box that behavior is for what goes on in businesses. It would be no different than if I walked into your [studio] this morning and screamed at you, 'Hey, you, put that mic down and come over here and get me some coffee.' You guys would have security all over me. That's not our atmosphere."

McQuarters denied that either he or his friend was loud in the dealership. "Nobody got loud," said McQuarters. "And there was no apology from anybody."

Mancuso tried to play down the incident. "We are not going to make a big deal out of it. We are just walking away from it. We want the Bears to do great. We want everybody to be happy. We have been in Lake Forest with the Bears for 21 years. We haven't built a business by throwing people out the door and disrespecting them. My family is starting year 81 in the automobile business. You don't do that [by] abusing people. But on the other side of the coin, we're not doormats either. We are not going to sit here and be screamed at and yelled at by perfect strangers. It just doesn't work that way," said Mancuso.

"I would never set foot in there again," said McQuarters. "It's a car dealership and everything in there is probably $150,000 and more. So if they see a guy walk in there with sweats and tennis shoes, they probably think, 'He's not looking to do anything.' That's versus a guy who walks in with a business suit and a coat and tie." —F.M.

I Had a Dream

Bears Pro Bowl kick returner Devin Hester said he dreamed of returning an opening Super Bowl kickoff for a touchdown. Not only did he dream it, but he lived it the next day against the Colts in Super Bowl XLI in Miami. Unfortunately, Hester could not do it all by himself and the Bears lost 29–17.

Former New York Jets defensive back and kick returner Earl Christy said he had the same dream and the same opportunity in Super Bowl III when his Jets upset the Baltimore Colts 16–7. "I dreamed about returning the opening kickoff for a touchdown in that Super Bowl, too," Christy said. "I remember seeing the coin flip at the start of the game and realizing I might have a chance to return that opening kickoff. I didn't return it all the way, but I had a good return. I caught the Colts' kickoff four yards deep in the end zone and returned it 26 yards.

"That Hester is amazing; he is the truth. But if you ask me if I would rather return the opening kickoff 92 yards for a touchdown or win the game, of course I would rather win the game."

Christy still insists that his Jets' 16–7 win—guaranteed earlier that week by Joe Namath—over the Colts was the biggest upset in Super Bowl history, even bigger than the Giants' surprise win over the Patriots in Super Bowl XLII. "The wives from the Jets and Colts were scheduled to play a volleyball game earlier that week, and people wrote that even the Colts' wives were favored to win that competition," Christy said. "It was very embarrassing. Nobody gave us any respect." —F.M.

Oh, Brother

Archie Manning, a former NFL quarterback, has watched two of his sons—Peyton and Eli—win back-to-back Super Bowls with the Colts and Giants, respectively. How cool is that?

Archie happens to have struck up a friendship with Dan Grossman, the father of beleaguered Bears quarterback Rex Grossman. Archie empathizes with Dan. "I love Rex; he is a great competitor," said Archie. "Rex and Eli are in the same era and they are at about the same stage of their careers."

Except that Eli now has a Super Bowl ring and MVP award, just like his older brother. Archie Manning said he sent a text message of encouragement to Dan Grossman several days before the Giants came to Chicago to face the Bears in 2007.

Rex starred at Florida before becoming a first-round draft pick, 22nd overall, in 2003. Eli was the first pick of the 2004 draft out of Mississippi. "We met Dan and Maureen [Rex's mother] when the boys were in college," said Archie, who spent 13 years as an NFL quarterback, mostly with the Saints. "Dan and I still communicate."

Archie opted not to come to Chicago to watch that Bears-Giants game, which the Giants pulled out with a second-half rally. "We don't go to away games anymore," said Manning, 58, who lives in New Orleans with his wife, Olivia. "We go up to New York three or four times, and we go to Indy three or four times to see Peyton.

"I love to see the boys, but I don't like to smother them. And I love my den and my TV. Going into the NFL for a quarterback, in most cases, is a yo-yo deal. They both have experienced that and are experiencing that. But they're tough kids." —D.J.

The Catbird's Seat

Rule number one for sportswriters: no cheering in the press box. But when the Bears travel to other cities to play their games, general manager Jerry Angelo and team president Ted Phillips often sit in the same press-box area as the writers.

While head coach Lovie Smith appears unflappable and stoic along the sideline—win or lose—Angelo has been known to express himself in the press box by pounding his fists on the desk, clapping his hands, shouting out encouragement, or slapping high-fives with director of personnel Bobby DePaul, as he did when the Bears edged the Arizona Cardinals 24–23 with an improbable Monday night comeback on October 16, 2006.

"When you win, everybody is euphoric," Angelo told me. "Nobody is that stoic. You are stoic because you have to stay the course and you have got to be involved in the game. Your emotions are always running strong. When you have a win, you are going to see that passion express itself."

Angelo admits to feeling a sort of fatherly pride when he watches the Bears from the press box during road games. "You are watching your kids and the fruits of your labor," he said. During games at Soldier Field, Angelo sits in a private box, away from the writers. "It's a place where we can yell and scream," said Angelo. "It's a sweatbox." —F.M.

A Bear Helps Katrina Victims

On the two-year anniversary of Hurricane Katrina, a storm which devastated much of the Gulf Coast, Bears defensive tackle Tommie Harris spearheaded a campaign to have the homes in New Orleans that were severely damaged by the hurricane torn down so that new ones could be constructed. The goal is to tear down 12,500 homes.

Harris says the precious moments he spent talking about football and life with Hall of Fame defensive lineman and mentor Reggie White will remain etched in his memory forever. The two men struck up a lasting friendship, and now Harris says he wants to carry out many of the humanitarian missions that defined White before his untimely death in 2003.

Bill Horn, executive director of the Reggie White Foundation's Crescent Rising program, estimates $25 million is needed to help rebuild New Orleans. It is great to see one of the young, current Bears with a solid sense of the importance of community involvement. —D.J.

Yes, Virginia

I can't recall a more inspiring sight than seeing Bears matriarch Virginia McCaskey smile while accepting the NFC championship trophy named after her late father, George S. Halas. The Bears had beaten the New Orleans Saints 39–14 to advance to Super Bowl XLI in Miami. Mrs. McCaskey, then 83, said she was speechless, but her appearance spoke volumes as to what the trophy meant to her.

It had been 21 years since the Bears last appeared in a Super Bowl, so no one in Chicago was taking this rare moment lightly. Tony Dorsett, the Hall of Fame running back, presented Mrs. McCaskey with the George Halas Trophy during the nationally televised postgame celebration.

Bears president Ted Phillips says Virginia McCaskey has expressed successor plans as far as ownership of the Bears. "I

No one was happier to receive the George S. Halas trophy after the 2007 NFC Championship Game than Halas's daughter and team owner Virginia McCaskey.

know that, first of all, the McCaskey[s] have been outstanding owners. They have shown great trust in me to make the right decisions on their behalf," said Phillips. "I am not an owner—I am the CEO. I know that they have obviously looked at their estate situation to make sure there is continuity of ownership. It is my understanding that they intend to own the Bears for a long time to come." —D.J.

A Crying Shame

Mike Brown epitomizes just how passionate a player must be to reach the highest level of professional football. The Bears' injured Pro Bowl safety is an emotional player, and his feelings flowed freely during Super Bowl XLI Media Day at Dolphin Stadium.

In the middle of my interview with him, after being asked how difficult it is for him to miss the biggest game of his life due to injury,

Safety Mike Brown has had an injury-plagued career with the Bears.

Brown broke down and cried. Brown had suffered a season-ending injury during the Bears' comeback victory over the Arizona Cardinals in October 2006. After undergoing surgery to repair ligament damage to his right foot, he was placed on injured reserve.

As his teammates and coaches smiled and laughed while they answered questions regarding the matchup against the Indianapolis Colts, Brown at first sat alone quietly, listening to music on his headphones. Bears players tried to make Brown feel an integral part of the team, even when he was on the sideline. When healthy and on the field, he displays excellent run-stopping ability, as well as general overall leadership for the defense.

Asked, finally, if the experience was bittersweet for him to accept, Brown's voice cracked. "Of course it is, man. It's tough for me," he said.

At that point, no doubt, Brown must have recalled how hard he had worked to get to this point in his career. He buried his face in his hands and began to sob.

What a crying shame. —F.M.

Number One in Our Hearts

One of the saddest duties of my professional career came on Christmas Eve, 1990, when I had to cover the funeral of young Bears defensive lineman Fred Washington in Denison, Texas. Washington and a female companion, Petra Stoll of Palatine, Illinois, died three days earlier in a one-car accident off Waukegan Road about 2:30 AM.

Barbara Washington had carefully wrapped two sweaters, a pair of jeans, and a bottle of cologne for her son to open that Christmas morning. Fred Earl Washington Jr., who died in Lake Forest, Illinois, at the age of 23, would never have an opportunity to unwrap those presents. But, his mother had decided, it was the thought that counts. And her thoughts, as well as those of more than 500 others who crammed into tiny Calvary Baptist Church, which seated 300 comfortably, were with her son.

Washington was due to arrive at Dallas–Fort Worth airport at 6:30 PM that weekend, and he was ticketed to return to Chicago at 8:30 Christmas night. He had sent gifts via UPS to his family in Denison. "He sent all of them except mine, because he told me he knew I wouldn't act right. He said I would get into it before Christmas. He said I would have been wearing it when he got here," Mrs. Washington recalls with a nervous laugh. "Christmas Day was always special to Fred. He thought he was supposed to be on the floor early to see what he got. He didn't like the shopping part, but he loved getting the gifts."

Mrs. Washington smiled at the thought of Fred opening the box with the jeans she bought him. "He would not have bought them for himself," she said. "These jeans are high-waisted. They turn down and have the belt loops. He would have said, 'Why did you buy me these things? You know I'm not wearing these.'"

On a crisp but sunny morning, Bears players Richard Dent, Terry Price, David Tate, James Rouse, Mickey Pruitt, and Dante Jones attended the funeral.

"Richard Dent was really sweet, and I have to mention Terry Price and Gina Rouse, James's wife," said Mrs. Washington. "She was a tremendous help. Her uncle owned the funeral home in Chicago that handled the memorial service the Bears held. I will be forever indebted to her."

Bears assistant equipment manager Tony Medlin, team president Michael McCaskey, and his father, board chairman Ed McCaskey, also were there to comfort the family of the promising second-round draft pick from Texas Christian University.

A day after the Bears' 27–14 victory over Tampa Bay, the team presented a game ball to Mrs. Washington with players' signatures and heartfelt condolences. Ed McCaskey represented the Bears in eulogizing Washington during the service. McCaskey told the family the Bears held a special memorial service for Washington in Lake Forest that was attended by all the players. He described how Bears players spoke through tears, asking, "Why did it have to happen?"

"Only God knows that," said McCaskey.

Earlier in the day, he handed Washington's brother, Anthony, who was six years old at the time, an "official NFL football" made of chocolate. Dozens of current and former TCU players were among the mourners, shedding tears, consoling family members, and recalling the good times. Players from Washington's undefeated 1984 state championship Denison High School team were there. So was TCU coach Jim Wacker.

Wacker said Washington was an inspirational leader on and off the field at TCU. "It was worth two touchdowns just to have Fred in the weight room during the off-season," said Wacker.

After the services, Washington was laid to rest at the Fairview Cemetery in Denison, some five miles from the church and 80 miles north of Dallas. A banner attached to a spray of flowers on the side of the casket read: "Fred Washington, No. 91 on your program, but No. 1 in your heart." That was a favorite saying of the Washington family, said his mother, who wore a banner bearing the same inscription. Washington was buried in the gray suit his mother bought him the day the Bears drafted him.

"His inspiration isn't dead," said his sister, Chrystal.

"I don't think Fred ever knowingly hurt anybody," Mrs. Washington said. "Even with his size, he didn't like people who picked on people and took advantage of their size. He always tried to treat people fair. He was a good kid. I want everybody to remember him for being the person he was. He was humble at a time when he could buy anything he wanted."

Bears coach Mike Ditka called Mrs. Washington and told her what a unique player and person her son was. "He said he never grumbled or complained," she said. "All that boy ever wanted to be is a football player."

Mrs. Washington, whose steady disposition was inherited by her eldest son, had been down this heartbreak path before. She lost her husband, Fred Sr., in an auto accident in 1985. He also attended TCU and played briefly with the Washington Redskins.

"Fred idolized his dad—everything just kind of followed the same pattern," she said of the cruel irony. "I don't think about it much because when I do, I feel like they followed the same path for a reason.

"They both succeeded in whatever they tried, and they met the same end. I think there is something there, but I can't figure it out. I guess it is not meant for us to know. So to keep my own sanity, I am going to stop trying to figure it out." —F.M.

Preparing for Battle

So what is Brian Urlacher's pregame ritual?

The Bears' stellar middle linebacker is a huge fan of fishing—something he truly enjoys when he's not playing football. Word is, every game day morning, Urlacher watches fishing shows on ESPN2 beginning at 8:00 AM. Right before he heads to the stadium, he eats two chocolate chip cookies and washes them down with a bottle of vitamin-enhanced water.

Whatever Urlacher consumes seems to be working well for him.

Throughout the history of the league, certain players have had peculiar rituals that they follow. Gale Sayers threw up before games on a regular basis, whether he wanted to or not. Among current players, Bears quarterback Rex Grossman takes a shower after warming up on the field prior to a game, and cornerback Charles "Peanut" Tillman has the same person stretch him and tape him before each game.

Miami Dolphins defensive end Jason Taylor is fanatical about doing everything from right to left, putting his cleats and socks on in that order, his wrist bands on that way, and brushing his teeth and buttoning his shirt. On the other hand, Tennessee Titans tackle Daniel Loper puts his equipment on from left to right for each practice and game. Giants wide receiver Plaxico Burress, who caught the game-winning touchdown pass from Eli Manning in Super Bowl XLII, eats grilled salmon and white rice every Saturday night before a game. Jacksonville defensive lineman John Henderson insists on getting slapped before each game by assistant trainer Joe Sheehan. San Francisco running back Moran Norris believes it is bad luck to walk under the cross bar before games. Redskins fullback Mike Sellers does not eat before a game, even if it's a night game. And Giants kicker Lawrence Tynes washes his car before every home game. —D.J.

Looking Good in the Lobby

All football fans know about John Madden's infatuation with recently retired Green Bay Packers quarterback Brett Favre. But I was curious as to who the NBC broadcasting icon considers "America's Team" at this point. Madden told me he thinks the Bears have a chance to become America's Team if they can find a way to win a couple of championships again. But until then, in his mind the Dallas Cowboys remain America's Team. Madden feels the Cowboys have more fans worldwide than any other team in the league. He measures their popularity by the number of people who greet the Cowboys in hotel lobbies around the country. Madden said there are thousands of fans in the hotel lobbies where the Cowboys travel, as opposed to 10 or 20 for most other teams.

He told me, "Wherever the Cowboys go, they are stars."

The Bears' attempt to regain the attention of the football nation may hinge on retaining coaching continuity. "The head coaching position, to me, might be the most difficult job in America," Bears president Ted Phillips says. "The business is built on wins and losses. Not to comment on any team in particular, but a lot of times teams are quick to fire their head coach, thinking that's going to be a cure-all, as opposed to taking a step back and taking a look at the overall structure of your organization, looking at the roles that different people have.

"Continuity is important. And continuity is important to me, as well. We are a few years into having Lovie Smith and Jerry Angelo together, and I think we are seeing the fruits of all those labors."

It is no secret that Angelo wanted then-LSU coach Nick Saban to take over the Bears before settling on Smith to fill the head coaching position several years ago. And it is likely that a minority coach such as Smith might have been overlooked if the "Rooney Rule," which requires all NFL teams to interview a minority during a coaching search, were not in effect.

Phillips says the Bears were fortunate that Smith was on their radar. "The reality at the time was that there were not many minority offensive coordinators or defensive coordinators. And there were even fewer college coaches who were minorities," he said. "So I don't think there was ever a conscious effort to avoid interviewing or hiring minorities. It was a small group to begin with. And we couldn't be more pleased that Lovie Smith is our head coach. I think it worked out great." —F.M.

Lovie Dovey

Coach Lovie Smith met his wife, MaryAnne Ford, on a blind date while they were in college at Tulsa. MaryAnne told me their first date was set up by her college roommate, and she and Lovie went to a pizza parlor. She was a sophomore and Lovie was a junior. As Lovie sipped on root beer, MaryAnne said she knew immediately that they were going to get married. Sure enough, the couple got engaged a month later.

MaryAnn grew up in Des Plaines, Illinois, and graduated from Forest View High School in Arlington Heights in 1977 before going to college at Tulsa, where Lovie was a two-time All-America defensive back. So when the Bears offered him the job as head coach several years ago, it was an opportunity for his wife to be closer to her family.

Mrs. Smith cites her husband's "integrity and his Godliness" as his two most outstanding qualities. She says he is a devout man and he is a very self-assured man. He has always known where he was going to go and what he was going to do.

In just his third season as head coach, Lovie Smith led the Bears to their first Super Bowl in 21 years. (Photo courtesy of Bill Smith)

Explaining her husband's unusual first name has been an ongoing ordeal. People often thought Lovie was just an affection- ate name she called him. But in fact that is his given name—he is named after his Aunt Lovina. —F.M.